WOMEN AGING
IN GRATITUDE

KIM KANE

WISE Ink
CREATIVE ★ PUBLISHING

ISBN 13: 978-1-63489-057-1
eISBN: 978-1-63489-058-8

Library of Congress Catalog Number: 2017936095
Printed in the United States of America
Third Printing: 2018
22 21 20 19 18   7 6 5 4 3

Cover design by Jessie Sayward Bright
Interior design by Kim Morehead

Wise Ink Creative Publishing
807 Broadway St. NE, Suite 46
Minneapolis, MN 55413
wiseink.com

To order, visit itascabooks.com or call 1-800-901-3480.
Reseller discounts available.

May you
always have
a reason to
sparkle!
　　—Kim Kane

"In the end, I think that I will like that we were sitting on the bed, talking and wondering where the time had gone."
—Unknown

It was always you, Pat . . . my husband, my best friend, my partner in life, my everything. This book is dedicated to the one I love the most, the one whom without I would not have always seen the possibilities of what could or will be. Your endless encouragement and ways of showing how determined you are to be that person for me can only be described as pure love. How lucky I am to have you.

And in the Beginning...

I HAVE LIVED MORE years than I have left to live.

I do not have a fatal illness nor do I have any mystical awareness of when I will be passing. But I know I have lived more years than I have left to live. It's basic statistics. Okay, deep breath, shoulders back, chin up (important if experiencing sagging skin), and let's think this through.

For starters, I'll just say it: I am a "woman of a certain age." I am over the half-century mark. I am getting older. I no longer wear high heels or small underpants. And while I never played tennis, I suffer from tennis elbow, in both elbows. I forget more than I remember, and I cannot read the paper without glasses. I can no longer eat anything with garlic or onions, or peppers, or milk with lactose, or (occasionally) peanut butter, for that matter.

The list of deficits seems to be getting longer as I age. I can go on for an endless amount of time about body ailments, not feeling relevant, not feeling valuable, and not feeling thin. When did this happen? When did I begin to fill an entire afternoon discussing colonoscopies and hip replacements? *What is happening to me?*

Pondering these questions and more was the original impetus for this book. Once I began to let it soak in that I was at an age where full AARP benefits applied to me and every doctor I had check-ups with was young enough to be my son or daughter, I began to wonder how other women were handling the aging process. I had my own stories about aging, but I wondered how others were doing and what stories they had once they hit a certain age.

I wanted to sort through my own experiences and, by doing so, gain some understanding of how I became older in what seemed like the blink of an eye. But I was also looking for companionship on this aging journey. I wanted to know I was not alone and that the experiences I was having, others were, too. I wanted to see if other women were experiencing a sense of loss around their relevancy and sense of belonging. So I decided to start asking around.

Turns out I am not alone in having questions and in seeking insights from others and I am not the only one wearing large underpants.

Once I began to ask other women of a certain age about their aging processes, it became clear to me that women like to talk about what we are going through, but we are not always asked to or given a forum for doing so. In my quest to gain more information and create a forum for this type of conversation, I decided to invite women to come together and allow me to ask a series of questions about aging. This was the beginning of "Celebrating Women" gatherings.

Celebrating Women gatherings offered me a privilege of speaking with over two hundred women, ages forty-five to eighty-five, over the course of two years. Some had formal education; some had little or none. Many had access to a variety of resources, while others had very few. I interviewed women living within the United States as well as some who had lived elsewhere. These gatherings were filled with Latino, African-American, and Caucasian women, all being asked the same questions about aging. To think this all started because I wanted to make sure I wasn't alone!

It became quickly evident that I am not. While this book includes a collection of stories and anecdotes about my own aging experience, it is also filled with the gift of words and stories from the remarkable women I interviewed.

I cannot adequately describe the way I was touched by these women or how graced I felt in their presence. I was enamored with each of them. Each left a heart imprint in me. As the movie line goes, "You had me at hello." Every single one of them.

From the sharing of other women, I became stronger in my own beliefs, my own "who I am," if you will. I also learned that being over fifty has its benefits for many of us. For example, we no longer care as much about the opinions of others, and we love having many styles of eyeglasses to pick from. We know who our near-and-dear friends are, and the ones who pretend to be. We have a strong desire to learn, and we see imperfection as an acceptable, even great, place. We need to have our story told, our experiences understood, and our love for sleep aids revealed!

From my perspective and affirmed by many of the women I spoke with, becoming a woman of a certain age can have some of the stereotypical drawbacks. In fact there is more achiness. And, yes, there is a slight, or not-so-slight, decrease in our hearing. We might make some unusual noises getting up from the couch. But aging has also allowed us to realize that, although we are getting older, our minds do not necessarily have to dim. Research indicates that our minds become filled with our accumulated wisdom—the kind of wisdom that illuminates our ability to make decisions without seeking anyone else's approval. We don't have to apologize for or ask permission to take care of ourselves. In fact, turning fifty and beyond has a freeing quality. Aside from a few exceptions, like wearing stilettos and crop tops, the sky is the limit to what we can do for the most part. Judging be damned, or at least limited. I want other women to see their ongoing potential and how they still sparkle.

After speaking with many women, I noticed a theme emerging. Aging, when mixed with gratitude, creates a perfect combination for living. For me, that idea became the perfect theme for a book—this book.

I began to understand the importance of sharing some of

the questions posed at the Celebrating Women get-togethers and including some of the answers given by the attendees as well. Many of the questions were like these: Have I lived the length of my life as well as the width? Why or why not? What am I most grateful for?

I hope that this book will help women see ourselves and each other as filled with wisdom and a sense of knowing. Wisdom of what was experienced as well as wisdom that is to come. Since 53.5 percent of Americans age fifty and above are women,[1] this means that on any given day there are quite a few women looking for where they parked their car. I want them to know they are not alone.

So look out! Many of us Baby Boomers are booming onto the stage, hungry and ready to make our mark . . . our second or third mark at that. We may be aging, but we are not done. Among the many opportunities for us is to begin to experience having our own time. Time to begin the next stage of our journey and re-imagine what our life can be.

In the beginning and in the end, my goal is simple. I want you to know there is so much more to come, to learn from, and to be grateful for.

1 See http://blog.aarp.org/2014/05/14/top-10-demographics-interests-facts-about-americans-age-50/.

"Dreams are renewable. No matter what our age or condition, there are still untapped possibilities within us and new beauty waiting to be born."
—Helen Keller

CHAPTER 1

Lions and Tigers and Hair, Oh My!

*The woman I was yesterday introduced me
to the woman I am today; which makes me
very excited about meeting the woman I
will become tomorrow.*

MY HANDS ARE OLD. I don't feel old, but my hands give me away. So does my neck and occasionally my eyes. And lately my hair.

I am not one to focus too long on things I cannot change, mostly due to my late-onset and undiagnosed ADD. But in the last five years or so, I cannot help but notice my body is becoming one big thing I cannot change. I look around and see other women who are aging. I feel hopeful seeing that women's bodies come in so many shapes and sizes. But I also know some of us are not so happy with the way we look . . .

or feel. I know instinctively which ones try to hide the years of accumulated excess and which ones who, at this point, really don't care. I am in between.

Many women I interviewed had no problem describing their own body changes. The range was quite large. Changes were from the color of hair (and not just on their head) to large, uncomfortable growths appearing on the side of their feet known medically as bunions, but sometimes referred to as a sixth toe. I was struck at how so many women used humor to speak about these changes. I found it refreshing. A common theme was extra weight around the middle. Honestly, extra weight in general made its way into every conversation, but tummy areas took center stage.

Jan, age sixty, shared how she used humor with friends going up to the cabin, which included the need to bring a swimsuit. Her response to being invited for swimming: "I'll bring the inner tube. It's easy to travel with, it's attached to my middle and never seems to deflate, and you can all hang on to me."

She added that she felt obligated to let her friends know that she might look like she had boobs in the front *and* back these days. She didn't want to alarm them.

Karen, age sixty-five, chimed in with, "This (pointing to her midriff) is not just a muffin top. I would be happy with that. I have a full-on loaf of bread."

Laughing ensued and several shirts were rearranged after she said that. Mine included.

Before one women's gathering started, two women were engaged in conversation. I overheard them talking about how hard it was to find pants that fit anymore. I jumped in and asked if they were experiencing issues with their middle area as they were aging.

They said "Yes!" in unison.

Two other women joined us and one shared how she really wondered if she maybe had a tumor in that area. To which another responded, "Oh the old 'I must have a tumor' theory. Check it out with the doctor for sure, but believe me, everyone in this room has thought they must have a tummy tumor!"

How I view my body comes and goes throughout the year. I am short. So for starters, I feel a little less fortunate than those whose legs are a few inches longer. What I wouldn't give for longer legs. It makes me wonder if longer necks would come with longer legs. What a dream come true! Truth is, a short torso came with my short legs. My middle looks like that toy my kids played with when they were little. You know, the one with different colored and sized plastic rings to stack on a plastic post. Well, that's kind of my body shape now.

Enough said.

The Proof Is in the Pudding . . . or My Hands

I can't hide my hands. I tend to be a hand talker. I use them to reinforce points or to reach out to someone and offer support. I use my hands to act out my words or draw people into my story. They look their age, and maybe even older than they are. My hands are filled with wrinkles and age spots. They tend to dry out after washing them and cramp up if used too much. As I age, I am more prone to having cracked nails and broken cuticles. Which is why, I suspect, a friend suggested I get a gel nail treatment.

"Oh, they're the best," she said enthusiastically. "You can touch them right away without smudging them. They will last over three weeks. Gels have been a life saver for me!"

Huh? I had never heard of gel nails, only acrylics. For me acrylics were a disaster and had everything to do with trying to look like a woman I knew who (I thought) was the epitome of a woman who had it all together. Nevermind the embezzlement charges against her. Acrylics were not for me.

I had a hard time wearing them and not getting my nails caught in car doors, breaking off unexpectedly (Damn, that hurt!), and poking through cellophane wrap. Just getting them re-done involved a nail tech wearing a HAZMAT suit and mask while I just sat there unprotected. Sometimes I held my breath, sometimes I didn't. No, acrylics never worked for me.

So now what about gel nails? Maybe this is what I have been waiting for. Nail polish that lasts, helping to make old hands look younger. I'm in!

An appointment for gel nails was made. All went exactly as I suspected it would. That is, until a machine was brought out and I was told to put sunscreen on my hands for protection. *For protection?* It was explained to me that having gel nails requires me to place my hands under a light similar to the lights used in a tanning bed. Not once, not twice, but three times for each hand. Well at least wearing a HAZMAT suit would not be required. The nail technician wore sunglasses.

I have to say these gel nails, or gels as I started to call them hoping I sounded cool, were really something I liked. It was true. I could walk out of the salon and do anything and not smudge them. I couldn't believe the freedom. I actually tried to smudge them. They held up. That is until week two, when the picking began.

As they do, my nails were growing and it was time to remove the nail polish. I had had a good run with the gel polish. I figured I would take off the old polish and go in for another set of gels. Only the gel doesn't come off. Really. I could not get the polish off. I tried soaking my fingers in a full bowl of acetone, wrapped each fingernail in cotton soaked in acetone, and, finally, I tried to file off the polish. Nothing . . .

I called my friend who first told me about the gels to ask

what I was supposed to do.

"Oh yeah, that's the tough part. I have to go in and have the salon take the polish off. It costs more money, but I couldn't get it off, either."

My friend had left this part out of the initial sale pitch. Suddenly gels were becoming too much work. I found myself feeling claustrophobic when unable to get them off, so I started picking at the gel polish.

That part isn't for the faint of heart. I picked until most of my nails bled. Two fingernails lost an entire middle of the nail and others became paper-thin. So thin that when I was down to the last two nails, I had to use an eyeglasses screwdriver to get the gel all off. I could not use my own fingernails to pick anything. Anything! My hands . . . well, my hands looked older than when I started out. It took almost two months to get back to the regular peeling and cracking. Mostly I wear clear nail polish now. Mostly my hands still look old.

All the same, my hands are the best way to get to know me. They were held out for my husband to take as we became married. They held his hands as we began our journey together then, and as we hold each other up now. They have held each of my children when they were babies, and even as they became adults. They have wiped away tears shed over losing toys, boyfriends, and girlfriends. These hands have held other hands as we have crossed roads, gone up slides, and then slid back down. They have reached up to the heavens to give thanks or to cry out *Why?* My hands have touched faces, touched lives, and made a difference for those who have had needs. They have cupped faces as love was expressed or a point was being made. I have used my hands to tell tales of joy or sadness and of experiences so big they needed something extra, like a hand or two. My hands will say "come here" or "go away" without any words needed. They bring people together, and they provide comfort. I have used my hands to hold another's as they left this world to go on to another. And my hands have brought me peace as I bring them together to give a prayer of thanks and hope.

Yes, they look weathered. But they look exactly as they should. Used, old, worn, and comfortable in their own skin. I will always see my hands for what they are. Ready for what is needed. Ready to show love. And always, always ready for a manicure.

The Cost of Gas

Being a woman over fifty allows me to speak of things I never dreamed I would talk about. Body changes, wrinkled hands, and, in particular, the production of gas. This gas is not the kind found under the earth or drilled for in deserts throughout the world. No, this gas is the one produced by me.

I used to be able to eat lots of different foods. I could eat at all hours of the night and each pair of my jeans would still fit by night's end. I never worried about what time dinner was served or the timing of eating a single food bite. I was always interested in making foods taste as good as they could, and that usually meant adding some garlic, occasionally some onions, and always something a little spicy. The more colors and textures in my food, the more the meal was enjoyed. And never, ever, did I worry about gas.

As I entered my forties, I will say that a few nights of eating out became uncomfortable. I noticed that my waistband dug in a little more, and my stomach felt and looked slightly pregnant. However, I managed to eat the foods I liked with minimal changes needed. Further into my forties, I became a little more concerned with the timing of eating. Anything after 7:00 p.m. became worrisome. I might not be able to fall asleep due to heartburn or stomach bloating. I had to think about that third glass of wine after 10:00 p.m., just in case. I also had to think about what I was wearing each day in case of stomach distention. No more wearing nylons or tights when out for dinner. No more tight-fitting anything when out for dinner, or lunch, or breakfast for that matter. I needed room to breathe and bloat. I took to wearing leggings under skirts with boots in the winter. Stretchy leggings.

Since the moment I turned fifty, I no longer have control of my digestive system. It controls me. I find that I need to eat before 6:00 p.m., and all foods must be void of garlic or onions. I am no longer able to eat anything fresh unless it's steamed first. My delight in spice is now watered down to salt and, sometimes, pepper. I no longer have much color in my meals. I am, in fact, eating more beige food. After every meal there is a concern: *Will this food I just ate upset my stomach?* or *Do I have any Gas-X left in my purse?* Or worse, *How loud will my stomach sound after eating?* Even worse yet, *Will I have any ability to release the gas if necessary?* After all, no one likes an older woman tooting along as she walks in public, right?

I have much to think about now regarding food, eating, and releasing. Currently, if I eat salsa at all, I lightly dip my tortilla chips and shake off any possible excess before I eat them. Depending on the night, this very lightly coated chip with mild salsa could cause a problematic digestive issue. Mostly gas.

I have gone to the doctor about this. On the way in the car, I practiced what I would say to the doctor about my gas and bloating. I sounded very mature and inquisitive as I practiced. But what came out to the doctor was, "I have gas, and it upsets me." Quickly followed by, "This has to stop. I simply cannot continue on like this. Please. You have to help me!"

Fast forward to the end of the conversation, and I was relieved to find out how normal this is, especially for women my age and older. For the record, it is never fun to hear "For women your age and older . . ." in any sentence, much less something to do with a medical condition. I think this should be taught to doctors in a sensitivity training course during medical school.

Back to gas. I do remember my older aunts making noises after eating. We figured they couldn't hear that they were tooting . . . or even knew they were anymore.

A woman named Sharon, age sixty-six, shared that one of her greatest fears is that she will get the walking farts. The farts where you toot with every step.

Understandable fear.

I felt somewhat relieved and somewhat upset at the news that almost every woman over fifty has problems with gas and bloating. I wasn't alone. The really bad news about this: that is a lot of gas walking around! The really good news about this . . . honestly, at the moment I can't think of anything.

The doctor recommended exercising to help reduce gas and keep things moving through, if you know what I mean. What I don't really think the doctor thought through was how awkward exercising with gas can be. I mean, think about it: moving my body about while it is trying to release built-up gas. I can only think of problems here. I am seeking other opinions.

Things I Am Allergic To

Having a body that fluctuates with each food item eaten, each weather change, or the time of day makes it a challenge when deciding what to wear. Clothing brought up a great deal of angst with many of the women I interviewed. The subject was usually met with heavy sighs and stories of unending drudgery, trying to find clothes that fit. Many things had to be taken into consideration.

Lisa, age fifty-five, shared, "I don't know how to take it when an eighty-year-old woman and I are looking at the same outfit!"

Chelle, age forty-nine, added, "It's hard to find clothing that fits everywhere you need it to. Plus, some fabrics are not meant for older women. Anything labeled 'Dry Fit Wear' clings, and you end up showing off places you don't want to emphasize. I won't wear that fabric."

Good note to self.

When I was younger, I never had clothes specifically to address different problems. I simply wore what felt right. I fit into everything I had. I would like to blame allergies for not fitting into all of my clothes anymore. If we think about it, having allergies causes people to react negatively to various foods, climate, and small, flowing particles. These reactions can be anything from red blotches on our skin, small red rashes all over, breathing difficulties, and swelling body parts. All are signs of an allergic reaction. I believe this applies to the wearing of certain clothes as well. I am finding that I have allergic reactions to certain clothing items, such as the red marks left by the belt that felt too tight or the short breaths taken while holding in my stomach due to wearing something that clings to my belly. Or the itchiness on skin caused by tight-fitting shirts or any tag left uncut. Or the swelling/bloating associated with wearing tight underpants or any garment really that is too tight. I am now certain these things are all allergic reactions as described by the *Journal of the American Medical Association.*

All things to be cautious about.

These reactions help to explain why I no longer wear hard-to-zip-up pants unless covered by a very loose sweater. The loose sweater helps with the allergic reaction I have when I have to unbutton my pants to feel better.

In my thinner days, I wore belts on my pants. That meant pants with zippers and belt loops. Zippers I could zip all the way up and waists small enough that I could fit a belt around. I am allergic to all of those items now. Out of sheer protection and caution, I only wear elastic waistband pants. I don't want to have any allergic reactions. I believe in safety first. I also wear lightweight skirts with elastic waistbands and all-cotton blend, breathable tops.

In addition to my current, allergy-free wardrobe, I have bathing suits with extra lycra material and attached skirts, and two full-length cover-ups. One bathing suit is black; one is multiple colors. I wear the black one. It fits me better. By "fits me better" I mean it doesn't allow for certain body areas to be as free as they would like to be, or certainly try to be. I am held in at just the right spots, and I am guessing a woman over fifty designed these bathing suits. Plus, when I have had enough of being held in, I put on the cover up. I usually follow with, "I'm a little cold," or, "I'm getting sun-burned." I let out my breath.

In a Celebrating Women gathering, Chelle, age forty-nine, brought up bathing suits she has tried wearing. "The ones with skirts don't really work for swimming. They are great for walking around the water, but once you are in the water the entire skirt flies up to the top of the water looking like a messy floating device around your face. The entire area I wanted covered is now completely exposed. It doesn't make sense."

Yet another reason for not exercising.

Having a belly that not only grows older, but bigger, creates a challenge in other areas. A woman I know named Nancy, age fifty-four, once said, "Belly fat . . . it irritates the hell out of me. It doesn't matter what I do to get rid of it. I've tried everything. Now I just see it as a badge of honor. I have been through a lot with this belly."

Nancy tells us this as she pats at her tummy. I find I am watching her pats create movements in her tummy area, and I wander into my own thoughts about getting older and having a bigger belly. It causes me to wonder if Nancy has heard about clothing allergies?

Honestly, it doesn't matter. Things change. Our bodies change. It's just the way this goes.

I tell people I am allergic to many more things now.

I have a box with a few clothing items I hang onto. I can't wear them as of yet, but you never know. My other, skinny body might decide to come back. In this box there are two skorts (in case they come back) and three outfits I would like to wear before I can't dress myself anymore. They are currently too small. But I have hope. However, I might be allergic to those skorts, so we will have to see.

There is some good news: ponchos are back in style this year! I say that to give merit to my purchase of five ponchos in the past year. They are the best items to complete my fall and winter ensembles. I have never felt such freedom in a clothing item before. First of all, I can wear any top I want underneath. By any top, I mean full cotton blend that is slightly loose, has no tags that will make my neck itch, and hangs in a way that I do not feel it against my belly too tightly.

Secondly, and probably most importantly, I can eat whatever I want, and how much I want, while wearing a poncho. It covers my midsection nicely, and all signs of bloating and full belly are blissfully hidden. It's like wearing Spanx, only it doesn't hurt! The trick to wearing a poncho is to find one that is not too close to a tablecloth in size or in any way resembles a holiday decoration.

The reason I mention the holiday resemblance is because I was talking with a woman at a wedding reception who asked me how I liked her new poncho.

Before I could answer, she said, "It's a Christmas tree skirt! Can you believe it?"

Inside my head I heard myself say, *No. I really can't believe it. What were you thinking or not thinking by wearing that?* Outside of my head I heard myself say, "Wow!"

I fake smiled as I walked away in my own poncho, suddenly wishing I had worn something different. And I am 100 percent certain I am allergic to wearing Christmas tree skirts.

The takeaway is, we must fight against wearing things that may call attention to our aging in a negative "you're going to be made fun of" way. Sometimes thinking it doesn't matter anymore mars our decisions. Yes, there can be a little bit of not caring as much as we get older, and that can be refreshing. But honestly, think it through before you wear an air freshener tree as a necklace.

I never wear anything that really accentuates my body type. On the other hand, wearing loose clothes may in fact accentuate my body in a way that makes it seem even larger. *Should I try wearing tighter-fitting clothes?*

The answer came pretty fast and resounded: *No!* This proclamation came with hands on hip and a look that speaks confidence and I make no apologies. (Well, there is one friend I secretly apologize to. To be discussed later.) I will wear only what feels comfortable to me. I have suffered long enough with too-tight waistbands and nylons that act as a vise around my swimsuit area. Simply put, I like loose, comfy clothes!

I believe my clothes represent more than what I wear. They represent who I am. I have lived parts of my life in clothes that itch and don't fit (all things I am now allergic to). As with clothing and in life, I have made compromises in ways that do not match who I am. By choosing to not live authentically, I had let others think I am not comfortable with who I am and in what I believe. My younger self wanted to please others more, to be accepted more by others. As I age, I am struck at the comfort I have in living life to its fullest in the way I want to. That means I can decide what works for me and what doesn't. I can wear purple tights with a green skirt and tie it all together with a lovely scarf (all things I am not allergic to). Or I can show up in sweatpants and tennis shoes and still be the same person who cares and wants to help.

As Linette, in her fifties, stated, "I used to think I had to wear makeup to go outside and garden. I worried I would see people and I wouldn't have on any makeup. Now it is so liberating to not worry so much about what others think."

In the end it is about our self and what we think that matters most.

I probably won't ever wear a Christmas tree skirt, but I am not ruling out year-round ponchos. I am not as interested in what others have for opinions on the way I do things. I figure the ones that judge me are scared to look at themselves. I honestly believe that what they think of me is none of my business. And I bet those who judge me are still wearing itchy sweaters. And I bet they are allergic to them and will still continue to wear them anyway.

All I know for sure is that I have found freedom in being

comfortable in my own skin, ponchos and all. And . . . I will never, ever wear too-small underwear. Ever.

Neither should you.

Mirror, Mirror on the Wall
(and not the one with the magnifying glass, please)

I do have one area I am slightly a bit vain about: my hair. I have been writing "groceries" in the checkbook versus "haircut" due to the cost of hair maintenance for quite some time now. And until I no longer dye or cut my hair, it will look like my grocery bill is quite high for two people every six weeks.

Hair is a pretty important feature for women. However, as we age, strange things start to occur. The once shiny, silky strands of sun-highlighted hair become somewhat wiry and dull. The highlights are now either something we pay for or are gray strands that appear more and more. After a certain age, the sun doesn't highlight our hair anymore; it only dries it out. Suddenly women of a certain age are wearing caps and scarves to cover up our hair.

My own hair has become a fickle friend. There are days I am thrilled about how my hair turns out. And other days, I have taken to wearing paper clips as barrettes to keep the wisps from hanging down too much on my face. I can't predict how my hair will look on any given day. I have also noticed if I don't have the right clothes on, my hair looks worse.

Having a bad hair day used to mean I had a small strand of hair falling out of my ponytail holder. Now I no longer have enough hair to even put it into a ponytail. It is way too thin. Having a bad hair day used to mean curls would fall by day's end. Now it means trying not to burn my hair (or other body parts) to make any curls at all. I had no idea hair could change this much.

I am breaking the secret . . . anyone under fifty: be aware that your hair will someday not be the same hair you started out with. It changes, and not always for the better. You will pay more money for hair maintenance than any other kind of body maintenance you might do. It's just the truth. Sometimes the truth hurts.

As we age, we know that society is not designed to welcome aging. All you have to do is turn on the TV to see commercials about defying age, wrinkles, and age spots. We do not place positive value on a woman's features as she ages. We are encouraged to do whatever we can to erase those lines, and plenty of products are available to help us!

Rita, age sixty-three, gave a nice summation to what many of us might think: "When I was younger I used to turn a lot of heads. I don't anymore. I think it's age."

It should be noted, Rita is quite beautiful. Still.

On any given day, I use up to four hair-styling lotions and potions. Some with spray tops, others with a pump, and still others with a squeeze top. I use them all together in the hopes that the one will stop the frizz while the other offers thickening, and others help with shine, bounce, and hold.

I have a routine. I can pump, spray, squeeze, and have my slightly damp hair (a tip I learned from a hairdresser) scrunched and spritzed all within a minute. It is something I take a little pride in. Every morning I play out this routine. And every morning I create a bathroom of hope. The hope that this is the day my hair will turn out.

And lots of times it does.

On the other days when it doesn't, I think about what else is on the market for hair care. I am, in fact, the perfect target market for hair care products. However, there are still places where we do not want so much hair.

"What is with all the facial hair?" asked Kathy, age sixty-eight, in a conversation she was having with other women. "I mean, I'm going to have to shave every day soon with a real razor. Not with just one of those cute ones used for 'sensitive areas,' either," she said, using air quotes.

She's right. I am convinced facial hair is where your lost head hair goes.

Facial hair is hardly ever discussed, but is not a very well kept secret. Many of us over fifty can attest to remedies for reducing facial hair only to find we are burned from waxing, broken out from allergic reactions to a product, or, worse, see dark pointy hairs replace the lighter, softer, barely there chin hairs we started out with.

A friend called me to ask what I thought she should do

to get the burned-on hair wax off of her upper lip area now that it had glued itself to her skin.

Many things went through my mind at this question. First, why did she ever think I would know what to do? Had she noticed my moustache? Had she known of my personal experiences with wax adhering to my upper lip? Had I ever shared my stories with her? I could not remember. But mostly I wondered if she thought I had a moustache. I was stuck between answering her to help out or to encourage her to call her doctor since, as I said to her, "I have no idea what you are talking about."

I mean, I like to think of myself as a good friend, someone you can call on in a time of need, someone who will be there through thick and thin . . . body type and experiences. But this. Answering this would be seen as a confession. So I told her to call her doctor.

To exonerate myself from not being a very good friend that time, and in honor of my friend, I will offer these tried and true tips when dealing with facial hair.

First tip: you need a really good pair of tweezers. This cannot be overstated. I have two good pairs. One is kept in my bathroom. The other is kept in my car. The sunlight and rearview mirror in a car provide the perfect match for plucking hairs growing in places we don't want. There is nothing quite like outdoor light. You tend to see things you did not see when getting ready using the bathroom mirror. It can be shocking. I am somewhat convinced that from the time

I check myself in the bathroom mirror, to the time it takes me to go directly to the car and check myself again in the car mirror, a dark, pointy chin hair can sprout. What else could explain how I missed that dark hair dangling from my chin? Honestly. Thus, I cannot over-emphasize the value of having good tweezers in your car. The lighting really is different. Don't be afraid. Just look. Keep in mind the same rules apply as with cellphone use: no plucking and driving.

Second tip: when waxing facial hair, always have a cooling cream to use after wax is taken off. There is nothing like getting your upper lip waxed and looking like Ronald McDonald afterward. Upper lip skin, or any skin being waxed, can become inflamed, red, and irritated. I recommend not having any special place to go to after this procedure. Or to see people you know. Or really, to see people in general!

They may ask out loud, "What is wrong with your face?"

You decide how you want to answer. And specifically to my friend who called me for facial hair advice, "Always go to a professional for facial hair removal. I really don't know what to do if wax adheres to your face. I rely on the esthetician I see to do it without burning me." I should have said that to you back then. Sorry.

Third tip: familiarize yourself with waxing appointment language. I make my appointments by deciding to call when everyone is out of the house, thus ensuring a better chance of keeping a few things secret. However, in the event that someone is around, try this: "I would like to schedule a brow waxing, please." (Somehow saying "brow waxing" doesn't involve as much embarrassment.) Then say to the person on the phone, "I would like an upperliponetoo."

Most people on the other end of the phone should know to say back to you, "Sure, wecanmakethathappentoo." Then they tell you nottopluckanyhairs before your appointment.

I love that there is a special language for this . . . it makes it so much easier!

Fourth tip: have a good friend who will understand the importance of not wanting facial hair to be too evident. This person's job is to mention if things get a little more notice-able and to offer a tweezers if need be. In addition, this per-son's job, should they need to, is to pluck any unwanted hairs if you cannot. They come to see you, ask for privacy to "visit," and then pluck away. In one particular women's gath-ering, Mary Beth, age fifty-two, shared that she wrote out instructions on a piece of paper and gave it to her husband should such a day come that she could not do the deed her-self. She doesn't have any daughters, but is hoping to have daughters-in-law someday. She has asked the note with hair plucking instructions be passed on to them.

I like her planning-ahead idea. Even if I am unconscious, I want to be sans any facial hair. I already have a friend assigned to pluck mine. I will do the same for her. Great tip: think about who you would assign this responsibility to, and be sure to let them know.

Facial hair for women over fifty is one of God's cruel jokes. On the other hand, with our eyesight fading, we tend not to be able to see it as well. We may miss a few hairs along the way and not care because we simply didn't notice. So maybe that's something to be thankful for. That, and scarves.

Does This Double Chin Make Me Look Fat?

I have noticed lately that the fashion industry has caught on a little more to what women over fifty are looking for. I have taken to wearing scarves, cute earrings, and updated eyewear. I have scarves in assorted colors and shapes. Some have fringe. Others have straight edges. I like the ones with thinner material. I do not sweat (as much) when wearing them. Or itch.

I like trying new ways to wear scarves. I have sites bookmarked on my computer to see how various people tie their scarves. I can take a good thirty minutes out of a day to watch people tie their scarves and then copy them. Or try to copy them. Did you know that if your scarf is big enough, you can wear it as a skirt? That is IF you want to wear it as a skirt . . . which I do not. Of course, if I am not careful, it can look a little like I am wearing a rug around my neck. However, if placed in just the right way, it can serve as a chin hider. It is all in the way it's tied. Really. I watched a video about it.

"I woke up, and one day I had my grandmother's neck. I can tell you I wasn't happy about it, either." This was shared by Debby, age seventy-one, as we talked about noticeable changes we were going through now that we had celebrated a few birthdays after fifty. "I never knew necks could wrinkle like this. I can't tell where my second chin ends and my wrinkles begin," she continued. "It's all blended together."

"Given your angst about this, do you try to cover up your neck?" I asked, holding my scarf up to my chin. My first, original chin.

Debby answered, "I don't do anything. I mean, what can I do? It is what it is, and I will just take it as it comes. After all, think of the alternative. I could have cosmetic surgery, but where would it stop?" she asks, holding her beautifully wrinkled hands. Debby looks down and ponders a thought for a minute. "I do wish I had worn more sunscreen, though. I am now telling my daughters to please wear sunscreen all the way down to here," she said pointing to what I think is her under-bra area.

She made a good point. Later, I think I will go out and buy a few more scarves . . . and maybe another poncho.

It's a Hormone Thing

I am always up for finding anything to blame but myself for whatever ails me. Lately, and for good reason, my "go to" blame lands on the hormonal shift that occurs with aging. That shift can be used for so many things. Eating too much? Hormones. Can't sleep? Hormones. Can't remember where I put my car keys? Hormones. I love it. I mean I actually hate it, but I love that I can blame some (most) of my problems on hormones.

I was having coffee with some friends when they began opening up about things happening to them now they were "women of a certain age." The conversation started with a friend turning red in the face. Actually it was her décolletage area *and* her face that turned red. Maybe a little blotchy as well. She asked if others were getting warm. No one was. Yet. We watched her go from a beige/ivory color to a full-on scarlet red. Her entire face took on a look of someone who was sitting too close to a fire and could get burned. She began to sweat, causing her cute haircut to look more like wisps of wet hair lying across her forehead and over her ears.

Needless to say, we all felt sympathetic. The rest of us took out our wet wipes, powder, and extra deodorant. One friend had a small fan in her bag. Of course no one mentioned that was weird. Years ago, we would have. Now we simply asked her where she got it, as if she has been keeping a secret from us. We didn't even ask about the cost.

Our friend was suffering from the famous "hot flash." If you haven't experienced it, you are lucky. If you have experienced it, you have my deepest sympathies. It is one of those afflictions that can literally be life-changing. All you know to be true about yourself changes. Hot flashes can stop you from going out, sleeping comfortably, and wearing only one outfit or pair of undergarments in a day.

Once our friend returned from being powdered and having an undergarment change, she described how she could be going about her business, getting things done, when all of a sudden it was as if a furnace switched on inside her. For her it began as a slow burn that eventually made its way to her head, causing her to feel as if she were on fire all over. It triggered her to turn red, sweat, and begin an unplanned striptease in places considered public. She hated it. It could last up to an hour before subsiding to a normal temperature.

As she went on about the embarrassing sweating that occurs, including her having to wipe down certain body parts, another one of our friends, Mary, age fifty-seven, gave her take on having a built-in furnace. "It's as if a water valve has sprung a leak. Only it's hot lava pouring out."

We all have our stories. We are all united.

Joelyn, age fifty-nine, added, "I can't take it some nights." Her face looked away, her eyes looked up, and she said in a voice filled with despair, "My bed is just drenched. I have sweat running down my face, and my body feels like it's stuck in a thermal heat wrap, and I can't get out. I have to change pajamas most nights. If I even wear pajamas. Mostly I wear T-shirts and shorts to bed. Not to mention I am washing our sheets all the time like I did when my kids wet the bed. It's exhausting. The whole thing is just exhausting."

We all nod. We all know. There are no more words needed. Hormones. *Hrummph* . . .

Hormones cause everything from hot flashes to vaginal dryness. From mood swings to not sleeping. To help balance me out a bit, I wear a hormonal replacement (HRT) patch. Please do not judge. I am very aware of all the latest and greatest research out there that speaks to both using HRT or not using HRT. For now, I will continue to wear my patch. Everyone should decide what is best for them.

A few women I interviewed offered their opinions and experiences about hormone changes. From Rita, age sixty-three, "I have been on a patch for over ten years. I am afraid to go off of it. I don't want to go through menopause."

Michele, age fifty-eight, added, "I even tried bioidenticals after I had a hysterectomy. That didn't work and cost hundreds of dollars. Now I'm on an estrogen patch. It seems to be working, but I'm worried about side effects."

Ann, in her sixties, stated very matter-of-factly, "I am winging it with hormone changes. As a result I only sleep four hours a night now. Hence the bags under my eyes. I wouldn't say it's working or not working at this point."

Suffice it to say, hormonal changes affect every aspect

of your life and, unfortunately, it is not a one-size-fits-all, nor is it for a designated period of time. Women interviewed shared stories about going through menopause for years. Some as long as ten years. One woman talked of daily sweating, fatigue, mood swings, and sleep deprivation for nine-and-a-half years. Yikes! I felt the need to start a Go Fund Me page for her just to cover the costs of all the products, medical tests, massages, biofeedback tests, and essential oils she had to pay for.

One common thread throughout each Celebrating Women gathering was talking about sleep deprivation and the possible link to changing hormones. Not sleeping took center stage in many conversations once the topic of hormones came up.

Angie, age sixty-seven, stated, "I cannot think of a time when I had a stretch of really sound sleep. I wake up in the morning after not sleeping soundly the night before, and my only thought is about when I can go back to bed!"

This exact sentiment was shared by almost every group I interviewed. This topic inevitably led the conversation to sleep aids. So many of the women I interviewed over fifty are either taking over-the-counter sleep aids or have prescriptions for sleep aids. I have no idea the exact number of women in general who are taking sleep aids, prescription or not; however, based on my conversations, I would offer the number as high as those who eat chocolate!

Sleep aids combined with pillows guaranteed for a perfect

night's sleep, or a mattress that forms to the body lined with a cool gel insert, sure to offer more than just back support, are just a few things available to fix what ails us at night.

True confession: I take sleep aids. I have for many years taken a prescription sleep aid each night before I go to sleep. I also have the above-mentioned pillow (actually two of them) and a mattress that can be adjusted by lowering or raising the air inside. I have a topper on my mattress that said on the box that it will provide support in all of the places I need for a good night's sleep.

But does this all work? No, not all of the time. There are nights when no matter how supported I am from my mattress or pillows, or the drug-induced slumber I am in, I still wake up. I never know the exact reason I wake up or even that it will be every night. What I do know is that once I am awake, it appears I kick in on all cylinders! The gerbil wheel of thoughts begin. All of the concerns, worries, things to get done, or a litany of "what ifs" make their way into my head. Unless I can catch that thing that clicks within me to fall asleep, I am up for whatever duration of time is left before the alarm clock goes off, thus depriving me of any further attempts to fall back asleep.

I am often perplexed about this extra time I have in the wee hours. Do I get up, start the coffee, and begin the day? Do I read? Do I start wash, clean bathrooms, and complete other tasks I don't seem to have time for during regular waking hours? I never know. I posed this question at the women's gatherings.

Sarah, age sixty-three, shared this insight, "Once I know I'm up for the day, I embrace it. I get up and start doing something. Once I'm on the move, I do pretty well and can hang in there for the entire day. If I get up and start to watch TV or sit around, I become lethargic and incapable of starting anything for the rest of the very long day ahead of me! The trick is to begin. I do feel lucky. I know that after two nights of not sleeping well I will sleep soundly the next."

My takeaway: one out of three nights sleeping should not be the norm. No one should feel lucky about this.

MaryAnn, age sixty-five, chimed in. "I lie there. If I can't fall back to sleep, I'm pissed. If I'm not pissed, I want to cry. Sometimes I'm so pissed I cry!"

Many women shared what they had tried or heard about to try for falling asleep and staying asleep. There are sleep studies to participate in, oils to rub on feet and hands, foods and drinks to have before going to bed, meditation, sound machines, breathing techniques, fans, Himalayan salt lamps to burn, eye masks, CPAPS and mouth guards to wear, journals to write in, and books to read. Someone always had one more thing to try! No wonder sleep-deprivation products is one of the fastest growing industries.

Another takeaway: when we talk about hormones, sleep deprivation is close behind. It is hard to sparkle after only four hours of sleep.

I take two prescribed pills at night. Every time my doctor

asks me how I am sleeping, I tell her, "Great, and please do not take me off of this prescription."

My doctor is close to my age. She gets it. I wouldn't be surprised to learn that she takes them herself.

In my early fifties, I was in for my regular routine OB/GYN appointment. I was examined by a lovely young doctor who made me feel very comfortable in what can be an uncomfortable situation. I mentioned to her that I was experiencing problems with some mood changes, hot flashes, and trouble sleeping. I was fairly certain I was experiencing perimenopause.

She confirmed that I most likely was and suggested a hormonal replacement therapy patch. She said her own mom was currently on them and spoke of how much better she was feeling.

Of course I focused on the fact that her mom must be around my age, thus, my doctor could be my daughter! She went on giving me research information about the safety of using the patches and talked of how she was very happy with the results from other women using them.

Here are the two things I heard the loudest that clinched it for me: First, using the hormone patch would help keep my skin supple, which potentially could help my skin look younger. She talked about how once you go off the patch and hormone levels drop, you cannot regain the elasticity you had when you were on them, thus causing skin to age. Once I stopped taking them, I could not go back on them. Second, regulating my hormone levels might help me sleep better. Enough said.

I am still on the patches several years later. I am assuming "change HRT patch every three days" will be in my medical chart when I am much older, along with "monitor oxygen levels." I have no intention of getting off of these patches or my prescription for sleep aids.

Another aspect of my younger years at the OB/GYN office was being in the waiting room, excited to talk about either being pregnant or becoming pregnant. I remember the camaraderie I felt with the other mothers waiting to be seen. We would *ooh* and *ahh* over the new babies or ask how the pregnancy was going. We asked each other questions in a way that gave us all a sense of belonging. We had bodies that were youthful enough to still have youth! It was a great bonding time.

Now when I am in the OB/GYN waiting room, I am still surrounded by young moms with newborns and toddlers. I am on the outside looking in. Those of us without young children or who aren't pregnant tend to sit quietly or occasionally ask the young moms how old their child is. Most of the young moms have ponytails, no makeup, and still end up looking like an ad for *Young Mothers* magazine. However, in this example, maybe I didn't look like they did when I was younger. I seem to remember big hair, rather large glasses, and frosted pink lipstick.

Moving on.

As I sit in the waiting room, I find myself looking for my reading glasses and something to read to keep busy and not seem like I am waiting for someone to talk to me. My magazine selection is very limited. I am to choose between *Parent* and the *Aging Well* magazines. I could also read a brochure about vaginal dryness and the new research about the hormone replacement patches. Or I could read about parenting a toddler and how to keep sexy time alive in a marriage with young children. Given my selections, I peruse my cellphone, wishing the younger women could notice that I know how to look at Facebook and can even upload a picture from my phone if I want to. This helps me feel relevant and current in a room where I don't seem to be. I find I still want to be seen as able even in a waiting room. Because I am, even if I do want to read about vaginal dryness. I also know a secret they do not know yet (keep reading).

I am reminded of my friend's comment about wishing I had known her husband when he was younger. I guess there is some truth to that for all of us.

In hindsight, here is my lesson learned: I am aging, and so is my body. It is that simple. Sure there are things to do to help my body look and feel better, but, honestly, nothing will stop me from aging. Nothing (insert heavy sigh).

I am a woman of a certain age, and each tomorrow will bring me to a place of being a little older. And I still want lots of tomorrows. I want to know that I lived my life in a way that had very little to do with what I wore for face cream or makeup. I am smart. I am beautiful. I am kind. And I am getting older. And, and . . . I am also getting wiser! Turns out I look my best when I live my best.

So in the end, it seems to me the best skin care might just be from a life well lived, not from a plant found in the Himalayas. I still don't like wrinkles, though.

The list of things that afflict us as we age is endless. There is the frozen shoulder syndrome, tennis elbow, and the need for mouth guards, support hose, panty liners, adult diapers, and control-top anything. There is the need for at least five pairs of reading glasses, a notebook to write where the reading glasses are, liquid tears for eyes that are dry, tissues for eyes that water, and face and body powder, just in case.

The list can get pretty long for ailments and body changes occurring after age fifty. Throw in hormone changes, and all bets are off for what could be on the list!

So here is the secret I know (that younger moms in the OB/GYN waiting room may not): we will all experience a multitude of twists and turns with regard to our bodies as we age. Our bodies continue to change, and not always for the better, no matter how many exercise classes we take. Some changes will bounce in and out of our lives for only moments. Other changes will dance with us for the rest of our lives. And it is all okay. No matter how we experience the changes, we will never be the same women we started out as. Nor would we want to be. I promise.

Many Stories Have Been Written About Route 66

There is a story for why the ripple of marks cover my lower belly area, looking like waves washing against a shore. They are silver and brown and sometimes look like ash. They are the marks that remind me of carrying each of my children inside my womb for what seemed forever, but is now remembered as a blink of an eye. They are the left-behind markers looking like a road map of excitement as my babies grew inside of me. The rippled marks remind me of the unexpected growth created by having a child inside me. Every time I thought I simply could not grow anymore, my body surprised me, and it grew even bigger. Those appropriately named stretch marks are also reminders of how much I stretched myself to be a better person. After all, I was going to be someone's mom. Someone's everything. I see my stretch marks as a story. Each story begins with love. At the moment, I do not have an end for any of these stories or marks. They are all still being written.

So I carry some extra weight and stretch marks run across me like Route 66. Knowing I will never again wear a size six, eight, or possibly even a size ten, I am still grateful. I tinkle when I laugh, or cough, or even walk too fast, and I am happy when a medium fits. I have also allowed myself to move on from thinking I need to be anything but what I am. I think one of the greatest pieces of wisdom women can learn as we age is knowing that we will not be perfect in any sense of the word and, in turn, that is what makes us perfect! There are no more illusions about what we need to be.

I no longer look to others to decide what I wear or what I eat. I now look to myself to be comfortable and healthy. After all these years, I know what works for me. I can only offer suggestions, not absolutes, for others. This is freeing.

As one of the women I interviewed said, "I have been choosing to be nonjudgmental. I realize others can live the lives they want, and so can I."

Exactly.

I no longer want others to remember what I wore. Rather, I want others to remember how I made them feel. I want them to remember that I was comfortable already, and they only had to get comfortable themselves. Yes, I still experience the ups and downs of weight, gas, and facial hair. But what I have also learned is that when you add a little humor to those stories and experiences, they add something versus take something away.

I live a fun and funny life. I still do not always remember where my latest pair of reading glasses are, or if I paid a bill some months. What I do remember is this: I am happy. I am filled with joy and gratitude so strong that even if I do find a black, coarse chin hair hanging so low it moves in a wind gust, I am not set back.

There are bumpy places on this body of mine. The bumpy places fit into my husband's bumpy places perfectly. Together we make a perfect road map of our life. There are fluffs of stuff that come out places I wish they wouldn't, but it helps to make me the imperfect-perfect woman I am.

Our bodies tell stories in ways that no words are needed. We have only to look at ourselves and see the beautiful transformation of our lives. We are beautiful now, and we will be beautiful later. We may gain weight, wrinkles, and have unexpected tinkles, but we gain wisdom and beauty along the way as well.

In gratitude for every wrinkle, line, or extra chin—all of these and more tell the story of my well-lived life better than words ever could. I am comfortable now. And who I have become suits me just fine.

CHAPTER 2

✹ Accessorize, Exercise, Accessorize! ✹

*"If only our eyes saw souls
instead of bodies, how very different our
ideals of beauty would be."*
—Unknown

I DO NOT LIKE TO EXERCISE. I pretend I do. In my mind I try to conjure up an image of me effortlessly stretching to beautiful music, positioning myself in a stress-releasing yoga pose. I am not alone in pretending. I have also thought about running a half marathon to celebrate the milestone of my running each week for the past several months. I have thought about how far I will ride my bike in the summer as I take advantage of the many trails available for my biking leisure. Perhaps even a bike trip out west. How fun! These are all lies. Or would "fantasies" be a better word? Either way, I have never, ever liked exercising. I've never been good at it. And I made up the part about running for the past several months.

This doesn't mean I do not have all necessary accessories for exercising. Of course I do! That is the fun part about exercising for me. I have two yoga mats, one orange and one blue. I have several styles of yoga pants that mix and match with several yoga tops that mix and match with several yoga socks! I also have two bikes. One is considered a cruising bike. It is a white-and-pink vintage bike with a bell and basket in front. I love this bike. It is a heavier bike so going long distances isn't always the best. But really, with the lengths I ride, I have never noticed. The other bike is lighter weight, the color gray, and has an odometer and an attachment on the back for two storage baskets. You never know, I might need to use those baskets to go to the farmers' market and fill them with fresh bread, jams, and flowers. Such a beautiful vision! I might also need to store other accessories. Or snacks. Given my yoga ensembles, you can imagine I have several pairs of bike shorts that match several bike shirts that match several bike socks. I especially like wearing bike shorts under looser shorts. I would never wear just bike shorts . . . there are obvious reasons for me . . . and the person behind me.

Moving on to what I said about running. This next sentence is true.

I used to run. Really I did. Many of us ran in our early

years. Some of us even ran together. Only the truly committed ones are running now. And you have my deepest respect. Several women I interviewed spoke of the desire to run, but several body parts were becoming more comparable to the Tin Man from *The Wizard of Oz*.

I tried to run a few times in recent years. To my complete embarrassment, I had to stop. I simply could not make my body go in a forward motion any longer, and I had to stop to use my inhalers. Yes, there is an *s* on the end. I have two different inhalers I bring with me.

Having the inhalers gives me hope. Hope that I can take a blast and off I go. Lungs open up, and the wind is at my back! The truth? I am sucking wind and it sounds slightly like a bad whistle and asthma set to music. Truthfully, I sound this way with or without the inhalers. But I do have the cutest running shoes! These are multicolored, fluorescent, could act as a beacon in a snowstorm cute shoes. They go with everything. Which is why I like them so much. I am not limited to using them as running shoes. I have gotten compliments from others as I wear them, but my children have given me other opinions. I get the feeling they might think the shoes are a little young for me. Which makes me wonder if others are giving me compliments because they think, *Isn't she cute? That older lady is wearing multicolored, fluorescent shoes?* To be followed with, *How adorable!*

I choose to believe they are just cute and I like them. Nothing more to be said, really. Except I don't run.

Hip-Hop

I have been known to exercise class hop while searching for just the right class. It's what I do to feel like I am helping myself stay fit and youthful, but not really having much success due to a variety of factors. One of the problems is I never seem to find the exact, perfect exercise class. Or one I haven't been embarrassed in. If I hop, I hurt my hip.

I've taken Zumba classes. Had to quit after I rushed out of the class when all of the shaking and jingling caused me to have a little tinkle accident.

I also joined a spinning class. I hadn't a clue that it was a stationary bicycling class for crazy people. Everyone is on a bike, and you pedal furiously while the bike stand moves up and down simulating a rolling hillside. I hated it. I couldn't keep up and lost my balance as I stood upward on the pedals trying to pedal faster. Both of my inside calves had a jagged cut caused by the hard metal pedals with sharp (I would call them unsafe) edges scraping down my lower leg.

The instructor came over to see if I was okay and mentioned the water aerobics class starting next week. Maybe I could check that out? Maybe. But all I could think of was being in a swimsuit—ironically one thing I was trying to become more comfortable with wearing by being in the spinning class in the first place.

Marching to Victory

My inability to exercise properly is also demonstrated at my ear, nose, and throat clinic. I had an appointment for feeling dizzy—another thing I have since learned can happen once you become a certain age. The doctor explained that he could get a better idea of how I was being impacted by dizziness by having me perform a few tests. One test was to close my eyes and march in place. I haven't marched in place since grade school. It seemed a strange, silly test.

At the doctor's instruction, I closed my eyes and began marching in place. Or so I thought. I heard a loud, "Whoa" coming from the doctor as he grabbed my shoulder to stop me from marching right into the wall, full boar, with my eyes closed.

After that he said I probably had a middle ear infection, or I suffered from vertigo (as my marching was so bad). Lesson learned for me: don't march in place with your eyes closed. And I probably shouldn't exercise too often. At least that is what I heard.

Breathe in, Breathe out

I did give yoga a shot. I felt it was the right kind of exercise for me, and of course, for a friend to accompany me. It wasn't something I ever thought to do, but I was ready to try anything to help with weight loss. I figured it was softer on the body and anyone at any age could do this. Plus, I liked the idea of using my breath to relax me and help with body movement. Based on what I had heard, I believed yoga was the perfect exercise for me.

In preparation for a yoga class, I made the trek to a department store with my 25-percent-off coupon to purchase yoga pants, a yoga top to wear while exercising, and a yoga top to wear to and from the class over the top used for exercising. I also bought a thin, roll-up, orange yoga mat and a thicker blue one. Just in case. Both had a case. Seeing a cute water bottle at the check-out area, I grabbed that, too. I felt ready to begin my new adventure as a yoga participator. Accessorize to exercise! I was in it to win it!

As an over-fifty-year-old woman, I needed to take a few things into consideration. Such as, I didn't want to be in a class that turned up the heat during class to help you perspire more of the toxins out of your body. "Perspire" seemed an interesting word to use. I would think it is more like a faucet pouring out sweat! Exercising with the heat up, *no thank you!* I can hardly clean my house without sweating and that IS with the air conditioning on in summer and windows open in the winter.

I also learned that there were a variety of class levels for yoga. Some with words in the description that I had no idea what they meant. I decided if I didn't know what it was about based on the words used to describe the class, I probably should not go. So I looked for descriptors such as: beginners, new, seniors, everyone, and all levels. Using those descriptors I found classes such as: Yoga in a Chair, Yoga and Relaxation (where all you did was breathe while lying on the floor), and lastly, Basic Yoga. I felt slightly limited in choices. I continued my search. I finally found a class that spoke to me: Big Ass Yoga.

Big Ass Yoga was for beginners who were not very agile and did not want to worry that we might be the largest person there. Based on what I read, it sounded like a fun class.

I didn't want to be alone so I went with a friend. Turns out she also suffers from gas. We agreed to try exercising as a way to handle both our gas problems (yes, I said it) and possibly lose a little weight. When we arrived in the class, we felt good. We had cute clothes, new mats, and a pedicure. Yes, we were older women, but we would not go out lying down. Technically yoga involves some lying down, but we trusted the euphemism all the same.

In the beginning of class, the instructor assured us that what she would be teaching would be simple to follow, and we should pace ourselves in case we haven't exercised in a bit. She talked about stretching, paying attention to our bodies, passing gas, our breathing, and . . .

"Wait, what did she say about gas?" I asked my friend.

We both looked at each other, and we both had that look on our faces that said, *Uh-oh.* No way would I be passing gas in a class that was about as quiet as a library. I assumed my friend felt the same way.

My friend and I seemed to be very natural at yoga. We moved our bodies along effortlessly, stretching and breathing in rhythm.

"I really like yoga," I whispered to my friend.

She leaned over to, I think, say the same thing; only all I heard was the sound of a large gas toot leaving someone's body. Next thing I knew, we are both trying not to laugh, and this only ended with us laughing so hard we were crying . . . and tooting!

I. Could. Not. Believe. It.

As best as I can remember, I left. I know I grabbed my yoga mat because I still have it in the trunk of my car two years later. Turns out I was in the wrong class. The one I should have been looking for was "Big Gas Yoga!"

Fair Weather Friend

At this point, it should be no surprise that my exercising is now limited to walking. I am not alone as an older woman walking. There seems to be an underworld sign-up place that I have not heard about as of yet due to the amount of older women I see walking at indoor tracks, malls, walking paths, and around my neighborhood. Many seem to be on a mission and have a stride worthy of a marathon, along with arms bent at the elbow swaying back and forth in front as if ready to punch someone if they got too close. I find myself nervous around them.

The good news for many of us who just want to simply walk and enjoy the outdoors is that all of the outfits we have for other types of exercising can be worn while we walk. There are not many accessories needed for walking. I find this refreshing. It has been my most inexpensive exercise to date. That is, until I thought I needed a dog to accompany me.

I wasn't walking enough. This came through via the numbers on my bathroom scale, the elastic waistbands feeling tighter, and the sluggishness I felt in my digestive tract. What to do? Of course, the obvious answer was to get out and walk more. But somehow I managed to need an accessory for even walking. I needed something to force me to get out and walk. What about a $450 puppy?!

I absolutely believed that if I had a dog, I would, of course, get out and walk more. This was the proclamation I gave to my husband and to friends who would listen, so much so that even I started to believe it.

So after shots; a new kennel; two dog mattresses (he ate one); collars of varying colors and sizes; two leashes, one leather, one spring extended; a puppy coat; and boots (mostly for photos), I was ready to start my walking routine.

We got the puppy in January. I live in Minnesota.

What. Was. I. Thinking?

My fantasy of walking with my cute, stylishly dressed puppy never included below-zero wind chill. Nor did it include icy pathways that seemed to call out to me in a taunt-ing, enticing way only to laugh at me when I fell. My hands were cold, my feet like ice blocks, and my eyes watered like a running faucet.

I stopped walking the dog. I blamed my joint aches and pains on the cold. I blamed my chapped, brittle skin on the cold. I blamed my inability to walk on the fact that it was pretty dark outside, even at 5:30 p.m., and I didn't want to slip on the ice. And it was cold.

Yes, I look back at this and still feel vindicated for not exercising . . . it was way too cold to be out walking. I think I am more of a spring, summer, fall kind of walking gal, with several considerations.

A side note: the dog still gets walks. It is now my husband who walks the dog. Every day. Sometimes twice a day. I will walk with him if the weather permits, such as on a day with a cool breeze and the temperature range between 50 and 74 degrees. It can be limiting, but as I age, I really think I know what is best (insert that look that says don't ask me anymore about this). Plus the dog listens to my husband much better while on a leash. I think this walking thing all worked out for the best.

In order to make up for the exercising I had to give up for a variety of reasons, mostly not my fault, I have taken to parking my car a little farther away from stores. This causes me to walk longer distances. Of course I park farther away only in good weather. Or if I think the weather isn't changing. Which it could. So I tend to park a little closer than far-ther. Just to be safe.

When You Can't Do It Alone

I know I need help with exercising. I also know that, as my body ages, my abilities age too. I fear simply beginning to shrivel up and not being able to move. I must play an important role in keeping my body active. I also need to be held accountable.

Enter Fitbit.

My Fitbit was a thin rubber-like band I would wear around my wrist that had lights blink when I got closer to exercise goals I had set. It monitored and recorded the amount of exercising I did, mostly via steps I took in a day, the amount of water I drink, and the quality of sleep I get each night. The trick was to activate the Fitbit via an app on a smart phone or computer and, most importantly, remem-ber to wear it. The problem was, I had to remember where I put it first to be able to remember to wear it.

Which explains I had a Fitbit. I lost a Fitbit. It all happened within three months. I was very upset. I looked everywhere. I had four people at one time looking for it. No luck. I had moments of thinking I remembered where it might have been placed by me, but everything turned out to be a false alarm. It became obvious to me what happened. The dog ate it. It probably had something to do with me not taking him on as many walks as he would have liked. I never noticed it before, looking back; he was never around when we were looking for the Fitbit.

As I reflect on my now-lost Fitbit, I realize some of its downfalls. Like the fact there doesn't seem to be a place to monitor looking for other misplaced things on my Fitbit. Which is a shame. I really think I could wow people with the amount of exercising I was doing on a daily basis if it did. Going up and down stairs alone should get me on the Olympic Team. If only fretting, looking around, and moving everything on the kitchen table at least four times could count as exercise, I would be beyond fit!

Meanwhile, my biggest reflection is that I might be allergic to exercising. That would explain all the problems I am having. I have made a decision to throttle back on the whole thing. I don't want to get sick or have a reaction.

There are other ways for me to stay fit, like watching what I eat. This is a tricky one. For starters many a woman over fifty will tell you her stomach has become an entity onto itself. There are times when my own stomach can fit nicely into maternity clothes and look like I am, in fact, needing maternity clothes. It may or may not have anything to do with what I am eating or a lack of exercising. It is as if the clock strikes in the late afternoon and *poof,* I am almost unable to see my feet when looking down. It is a phenomenon experienced by many women, called the afternoon bloat.

So far this stomach-extending-hurts-to-breathe bloat is not recognized by any medical journal. However, given the number of women over fifty wearing elastic waistbands, I have no doubt it should be. Many women I interviewed talked of thinking they had a tummy tumor. (Referenced in other chapters.) What else could possibly explain still having bird legs, a bulging middle, and the inability to button your pants after 4:00 p.m.?

Alice, age sixty-five, shared that she insisted her doctor order an MRI to at least rule out a tumor. She was so certain she had one. A few days prior to the MRI, Alice had been looking online at what kind of tumors can reside in the stomach. None of them end well for the person having the tumor. She began to overwhelm herself with thoughts of having cancer and having to say good-bye to her family. She started to act like she, indeed, had a deadly tumor in her stomach.

Alice shared that the day of the MRI she was a wreck and had not slept the night before, given all of her worrying. She went through the test as if they would surely prove her death sentence. Close friends and family called to see how it went and each phone call ended with a variation of "I will pray for you." Well, by God, a miracle did happen! Alice shared with us she did not have a tumor, she was just getting fat!

However, the words she used to answer the question when friends and family asked what the MRI results were, "Inconclusive, but definitely not cancer."

Smart woman.

Fashion as we age does get a little tougher in terms of fit and comfort. Georgia, age sixty-four, said, "I now have to buy pants thinking if they will fit me before the bloat and after the bloat sets in each day. Half the time my pants end up being saggy in the legs and rear, but feel snug in the belly. Most of my pants waistbands are all elastic now. I don't even care what they look like anymore. I just want them to feel comfortable."

Another smart woman.

Healthy Eating and Other Lies I Tell Myself

Watching what we eat is important for a healthy lifestyle at any age. As I am typing these words while in a library, I look across the table to the bookshelves and I see a book titled: *Eat More Weigh Less.* Really? How dumb do you think we are? But I am intrigued.

I also want to believe the commercial that tells me I am not fat, I am just bloated and there's a pill for that. I open the book to find out that you can eat more and not weigh more. But there is a catch . . . you have to eat more foods that are really non-foods.

Let me explain.

The book claims that if you eat more lettuce (non-food item), certain other vegetables (non-food items), and limit your fat intake (this includes cream for my morning coffee . . . unacceptable), you will be able to eat more and weigh less. It also mentions something about exercising.

Moving on.

What I didn't see, but wanted to see, is how I could eat more bread items (wonderful food items), pasta (especially wonderful food items with sauce), and chocolate (lots of people consider this a staple food item . . . just ask them), and not weigh more. This is the problem. Until we start addressing how to eat the non, non-food items and not gain weight, healthy eating be damned.

Gail, age sixty-nine, spoke of another idea for eating better. "I just eat small amounts in increments throughout the day."

Someone asked her how many times a day she ends up eating.

"At least twenty," she answered.

That might explain why we notice her bloat throughout the day, not just after 4:00 p.m. No judging, just saying.

Here are a few tricks (lies) I have learned along the way and want to share.

- When going out for a meal with friends, say before you order the one-third-pound hamburger and fries, "Oh, I might as well get something filling. I won't be eating the rest of the day." You will feel better, and you will feel justified, regardless if eating later or not. Be careful, though—this type of food has been known to produce gas. Be sure to think this through.

- Eat oatmeal the "right" way. Place chocolate bits and nuts with brown sugar at the bottom of a bowl. Add your cooked oatmeal on top. Allow others to only see the oatmeal. Once you get to the bottom of the bowl, discreetly eat. Walk away if you can for more privacy. You may lick the bowl out of habit, but nobody wants to see that.

- Wrap your chicken fingers in lettuce. Or wrap any other breaded item in lettuce. The lettuce gives an illusion of healthy eating. No one needs to know what is inside.

- Always bring snacks to outings. If it is a sporting event, then of course you will need the energy. If it is another type of event, you can always say you are trying to save money. If you end up buying something at a concession stand, you can always mention your blood sugar. No one questions concerns around blood sugar.

- Anytime you are consuming alcohol, you will sound much more responsible if you say you want something in your stomach. So eat away. After all, it's the right thing to do.

All these tricks (lies) are dependent on the time of day you eat. There is a reason for those early-bird specials for seniors. We need time to digest food before bed. Consider your healthy eating plan to include eating four hours before bed, unless you are taking a certain type of medication that says otherwise, have not exercised for quite some time, drank too much alcohol, missed the early bird special because you forgot, got hungry after eating so early, feel silly eating so early, are bored and have nothing to do but eat something because you ate so early . . . okay, I am re-thinking the eat early idea. If that is your thing, great. But don't eat early just because you can. Eat what you want and where you want. Just be smart about it. Nobody wants to hear about your digestion issues later. Nobody.

Healthy eating has its place. It's just hard to do. Eating healthy really has nothing to do with age. It's just an age-old problem that follows us through life. I think the better lesson is to embrace who we are—all of who we are. If we need to make changes, we know what to do. We have been around long enough to know how and what to eat. Fine.

One Lump or Two?

Let's face it, our body takes on a different look as we age. We look for ways to keep ourselves fit and looking good. Our society does not make it easy for women to age. Even with exercising and eating right, we still want ways to look better. Which leads me to Spanx.

Spanx is a type of tight-fitting undergarments, used much like a girdle was back in the day. Only Spanx shape-wear doesn't require any hooks, buttons, or ties. Its main job is to smoosh in and smooth out bumps and lumps on our body. I would also add, to suck the breath right out of us. I have tried several types: full-body Spanx, stomach-only Spanx, and stomach and thigh Spanx. To be honest, two of the three have ended up in either a waste bin in a restaurant's restroom, or in my purse by night's end. The other Spanx was thrown away with underwear that lost its elasticity . . . ironic, right?

I will never wear them again.

I am who I am. As I have let on before, I have lumps and bumps and dimples and dents. As I look around, I see many shapes and sizes and others with bumps and lumps. It seems we are all put together in a way that is unique only to ourselves. However, some of us fight to look like others younger than us, thinking that is better. We worry that with age comes the loss of our beauty, the loss of our identity. The truth is, that is on us. We do that to ourselves . . . remember Alice? She believed she was sick with a cancerous tummy tumor, so she started to act as if she was. The opposite is true, too. What we believe is what we become.

What Matters Most

With all the many shapes and sizes, I also see many forms of beauty. It is in the twinkle of the eyes, the variety in the shades of silver and gray hair, the laugh lines surrounding a woman's mouth and eyes, and the confidence in her walk and stance. Beauty is all around me, especially in women over fifty. That kind of beauty and sparkle fills a room and brings a sense of confidence that can only come from experience and time. And it is time.

It is time to believe that no matter the food I eat or don't eat, the exercise I do or don't do, I am finally happy with who I am. After all these years, I get it. I want other women to know it and get it, too!

We will shine with or without the perfect body. We will love and receive love no matter our size. We will see miracles, have faith, and be a part of something greater than ourselves every day in spite of our clothing size or whether we wear a belt with our pants or not. To get to a place called Grace, and to see that we are just as important as the rest, is one of the gifts given from aging. It is not about gaining weight, but gaining wisdom.

So let's take care of us. We know what that means. We know the strength of our body and the way it needs to move. Over time we have learned how to accentuate the positive and draw away from what isn't. Change what we need to and accept what we can't. Our beauty lies within. No accessory or exercising is needed for that!

"You become. It takes a long time. That's why it doesn't happen to those who break easily, or have sharp edges, or who have to be carefully kept. Generally by the time you are Real, most of your hair has been loved off, and your eyes drop, and you get loose in the joints and very shabby. But these things don't matter at all, because once you are Real you can't be ugly, except to people who can't understand."
—The Velveteen Rabbit

In gratitude for finally becoming.

CHAPTER 3

✶ You've Got a Friend in Me ✶

"One universe, nine planets,
204 countries, 809 islands, seven seas,
and I had the privilege to meet you."
—Unknown

SOMETHING SO MAGICAL HAPPENS between women. There is a strong, powerful force that links us together. This force is never seen; it is only felt. It is the small tight knots that form on the rope that act as a lifeline.

Ask a woman to describe her friendships that are strong, and you will hear things like: "My friends are always there for me. Not always in the physical sense. I just know they are there, and that is enough." Or "I could call my girlfriends in the middle of the night, and they would say they were already awake and would talk to me."

As a good friend of mine always says, nicely summing up what it means to be girlfriends, "My friends are like my soul sisters. We get each other. We don't always need words, but once we start talking you can't shut us up!"

Total. Girl. Power.

Can You Hear Me Now?

"Can you hear me?" I asked my friend who was wearing her hearing aids for the first time.

"Yes, but I think you are too close. I want you to go farther away to make sure. Go over by the tires," she says in the large warehouse store with her back to me.

"That's too far," I insist. "Why is your back turned to me? You're not trying to guess if I'm talking, are you?"

"No, no, no, I'm focusing on listening. I've been reading lips for a while now, and I don't want to see yours. By the way, I'm not so sure of your lipstick choice lately. Try a lighter, softer pink."

"Really," I say with a slight edge to it. "Why didn't you say something earlier?"

"No reason," she says. "Can we get back to my hearing aids? I need to know if I can hear you. Go back by the rice and bean area. Don't yell, just talk normal to me."

I do. Since I have to talk, and she needs to test out her new hearing aids, what better time than now to ask what else she hasn't told me about with regard to my makeup choices as of late.

"Okay, can you hear me? I am over by the rice and beans

without any lipstick on."

"What?" says my friend. "Why aren't you wearing any lipstick?"

"I don't like it anymore," I say, a little wounded and with a fist of Kleenex and my lipstick smeared on it. I put a box of rice over my face to talk to my friend; after all, we are testing out all possibilities for hearing. "Do you like my blush color?"

"Talk a little louder with the box in front. And yes, I do like your blush. I just think the pink lipstick was too pink. You wore another lipstick last Friday. I liked it better. It was softer on you. Okay, can you go back over by the tires? Face the poster hanging up and pretend you are reading something."

I walk over to the poster, face it, and begin talking. "Oh okay, good, I'm glad you like it. Can you hear me when I'm facing the poster?"

"Yes, yes. I can hear you. This is good," said my friend, now walking over to the bakery area. "One last test," she says while adjusting her hearing aids. "Walk to the end of the aisle and call out my name. Let's see how that sounds for me."

"Gail, can you hear me?" I say in the voice I might have used with one of my children when they were younger.

"Wonderful! Yes, I can hear you! Oh, this will be so much better for me. The whole world just opened up. By the way, where did you get your blush? I really do like it."

"Yay! You can hear!" I say happily for my friend and really mean it, forgetting all about any worries around my lip or cheek color.

Luckily, I realized with a great sense of happiness, a friend will tell you the truth about lipsticks and anything else you ask her about. I also realized a friend knows when it isn't about her anymore and stops talking about herself, including asking about lipstick and blush color.

"You know, ironically, you are a friend with whom words aren't always necessary." I say to her, knowing she can now hear me without any hesitations or guesses, "I don't have many of those friends. All the same, I'll have to be careful what I say around you now. You'll hear every word."

She winks at me.

I smile back and place my arm through hers. I feel so happy for her. I feel so happy for me. Yep. Total girl power.

That is what friends do. We make sure our hearing aids work and our lipstick is just right. It's all about creating the knots on our lifeline rope throughout our life. As we age, we continue to bring strength to the knots of our friendship. Friendship that creates those knots will continue to grow right through whatever comes our way. This is the rope to hang onto in life . . . the one with all the tight knots on it. Our friendships' strength is found in those knots. Our lives' strength is found in those knots.

A woman I interviewed said this about friendship: "Surround yourself with people you want to be with. Don't waste time with others you don't feel good about. Examine people in your life to see if they fill you up or take away."

This sentiment was shared by several women I interviewed. The belief in sharing space only with those who lifted you up was a common theme. It became evident that many women over fifty did not want to have too many people in their lives who took energy away from them. It seemed that looking back helped to give clarity around how women wanted the future to look, and there wasn't much room for life-suckers, people who squeezed the life right out of you.

Another piece of wisdom shared in a variety of ways by a variety of women I interviewed was put most eloquently by JoAnn, age seventy. "Learn to love people for who they are, not who you want them to be. When people tell you about themselves . . . believe them. Listen to what they say. Watch what they do. Offer your support to friends, not your advice."

When she spoke there was a sense of having been there. She is a seventy-year-old woman who has a wealth of knowledge and vast experiences I am certain we can all learn from. When she spoke I could not help but feel like I was listening to a mentor. By sharing her words in this book I hope she becomes a mentor to many.

I bought a friend a barometric pressure measuring device. I can't think of the name right now (or maybe that IS the name of it). It has some sort of fluid in a long, tubelike container that has several multicolored floaters. Based on where the floaters are in the liquid, it tells you if the barometric pressure is going up or down. Going up can mean sunny, warm, humid days. Floating at the bottom can mean storms are likely coming, and that can also mean warm, humid days. So obviously we want the floaty things to be somewhere in the middle. I thought it was a fun gift for my one friend having another midlife birthday. She did not.

"This measures humidity? I don't want it," my friend said indignantly. "Why did you get me a gift that will anticipate when humidity is in the air? Isn't it enough to wake up and just know?"

I watched her wring her hands together as if I gave her a time machine telling her the date of her death.

"I already know when I wake up if there is humidity. My hair is limp and wispy, and my sheets are even more soaked than normal. Not to mention my night face cream has not soaked into my face even after seven hours of having it on." She pushed back a stray, gray hair strand, seeming to gain composure. "So. I really do not need an apparatus in my home mocking me with its floaty things telling me, haunting me that it will be humid out!" She takes in air loudly.

I am silent. I am silent because she is right. Everything she says is right, and I still bought it for her. And worse, I knew. Of course in my mind I had inserted the word "prepping" instead of "mocking." Nonetheless, I felt awful and exposed.

This gift faux pas gave my friend and me something to bond over. So much so we only need a few words to discuss it anymore. There are certain days I will text her only one word: humid.

She responds, "I know." No need for more. We both know what we mean.

Ah, to have such good friends! Another tight knot on the rope of life.

Then there is the tight knot you get in your stomach. The one when someone pretends to be your friend. But really isn't.

I pride myself on sensing genuine people and potential good friends. I seem to have a spidey sense about people and whether we will be a good fit as friends. When this sense is challenged, I become out of sorts. My game is off.

We all know there are universal friendship codes in place. When any of these is broken, life becomes tilted. Fortunately there are checks and balances in place for a breach. Fortunately there are the girl friendship codes to keep things straight.

Girl Friendship Codes

These girl friendship codes are a glue that holds us together. Having codes allows us to keep order in a way that isn't designed to create problems, but rather to keep friendships strong.

If a code is broken the first time, everyone gets a break. We move on. If the code continues to be broken, changes are to be made, and sometimes friendships cease. With each friendship, there are often a variety of codes in place. Each friendship has a unique offering that needs its unique set of codes. Codes will change as our age and expectations change. To get a better sense of this, let's review a few girl friendship codes.

No Lying . . .

One of the most important codes is no lying. There are a few caveats to this one. Not being honest (nicer way to say it) may include discussing a topic causing great pain for the other person. For example, if your friend shares that her husband is leaving her for another woman, do not offer reasons why that might be happening, even if asked.

And if she asks, only focus on how awful her husband is behaving. If your friend insists on discussing the other woman and how she is younger and thus has perkier body parts, no need to agree. Redirect. Focus only on the friend's attributes, even if she insists on bringing up her underarm fat. Remind her there are sleeves for that.

Being honest with our girlfriends is what keeps us trusting each other. I mean, who doesn't appreciate hearing from someone you trust that maybe those new eyeglasses could be exchanged for a new pair before the return policy expires. Or perhaps next time when you go to the hairdresser you don't have to walk out with such large blond streaks. If we can't tell our closest friends what is what, then maybe the friendship isn't as tight as we think.

Being honest can be tough. I had someone once sit me down and tell me I needed to stop wearing such big, loose-fitting clothes. She was kind, thoughtful, and had no malice in her voice as she said it. Only problem was I wanted to punch her in the face after she said that. Hard.

To this day and probably because of that, she is one of my dearest friends. I trust everything she says, and I find myself actually asking for her opinion. Refreshing. It should be noted that on occasion I do wear big, loose-fitting clothes.

However, I try not to when I am with her.

No Judging . . . (for the most part)

If a friend calls and leaves a frantic message to call back, you call back without judging how high her voice is shrieking. When a friend stops by without calling first, assume she needs to see you. Make the time. Believe she needs to talk with you without you judging. If a friend says she is so sick and tired of her children she wants to tie them all up and put them in a closet for two hours for some peace and quiet, laugh and say, "I know what you mean." Don't call child protection. Unless she has tied up her children before and put them in a closet. Then call child protection while on your way over to her house.

This involves using good judgment and a little bit of "raise of the eyebrow" judging.

Having a friend that does not judge us is a gift. This is the person we can meet up with and wear our sunglasses the entire time we are together, whether it is due to a recent Botox appointment, allergy, sensitive, dry eyes, or the simple fact we chose not to wear any makeup. There is no judging. We want friends who will understand that we may not always be our best selves. This may come in the form of memory loss, hearing loss, eyesight loss, hair loss, and the ways we handle loss. All of it is taken in stride. None of it means we are not worthy of having friends.

On the other hand, what we do need in a friend is the ability to ask the tough questions without judging. A good friend is not one that will gloss over the tough stuff. No, she is there when things do get tough and for when some re-examining of how situations were handled is necessary. She confronts without being confrontational. She does this without judging.

A great illustration of this is from a lunch with a friend. I began to lament after feeling I was not being understood by someone regarding a project I was working on. I wasn't feeling relevant anymore. As I interviewed other women, I came across a few others who were feeling the same way.

Carolyn shared, "Sometimes I look around the room and I could be a parent to most of my colleagues. And I don't feel like a colleague anymore. I just feel old."

That was how I was feeling about my project.

Without any accusatory tone, my friend asked me a few questions. She asked me to state exactly what my desired outcome was. She asked me to think through all of my options, to check if I was assuming others would have the same interest and would give the same kind of value to this as I did.

At first I was taken a bit off guard by her questioning of my process. I kind of wanted her to lament with me about ageism, and how we were still capable and smart. I wanted her to feel the indignation I was feeling and join me in blaming others. But then I realized her intention was coming from a good place, and one that was to move me forward; her questions became my guide as I worked toward my desired outcome for the next several weeks. She stayed with the code of "No Judging," and she was still able to move me out of my pity party.

Keeping Secrets. Keeping Trust.

I have had a friend for over forty-seven years. I would trust her with anything, and I do trust her with ANYTHING. We have shared things with each other that we would not tell others. We have told each other things so personal that our rope lifeline is filled with knots so tight that when you tug on it, it only becomes stronger. And sometimes we hang on hard to that rope lifeline, pulling us out of this or that.

Unfortunately, I have also made friendships with no-rope

lifelines. I have trusted too quickly and without listening to the beautiful intuition that whispered: "Be careful." This lesson learned was demonstrated out loud and in public.

"Hey, do you still write a grocery store name in the checkbook register when you get your hair cut and colored so your husband doesn't know?"

This question was delivered to me at a dinner party from someone I thought was a friend. The dinner party guests included my husband and some people I did not know very well. This question was loudly asked, and a laugh was added.

Now there are many things to be gleaned from this simple question. One, this is not a friend. Friends know not to ask questions about secrets shared in private while you are in a public setting or when spouses are present. They will have broken a code. And they certainly do not ask and then add a laugh. The laugh suggests calculation and insinuates a "Gotcha" moment. Everyone knows that. Everyone else knew that at the dinner party.

Two, I am reminded of the saying, "Keep your friends close and your enemies closer."

I will forever watch what I say to this person. How could I not? A security breach has occurred, and it is all hands on deck. The friendship needs to be exposed. My younger, need-people-to-like-me self was more likely to defend and try to explain. I would be the one to look foolish. Only this time I am wiser (score a point for age).

Which brings me to number three. I am too old for this

shit. I do not need people in my life to call me out on anything. So I did what felt to be the right thing at the right time and what I would have done in kindergarten (because nobody likes a tattletale): I put her in her place. Or a nicer way to say it, I simply answered her question with a question.

Eyebrow raised, head cocked to side, I said, "I think you are asking about the idea I gave you when you said you didn't want Tom to know how much money you were spending at the salon. I suggested you write the grocery store name in the checkbook. How is that working for you?" And then, "Tom, did you ever figure out that little trick?"

I smiled, took a sip of wine, mentioned how yummy the food was, and moved along. Just like that friendship should. And has.

"Don't mistake my kindness for weakness. I am kind to everyone. But when someone is unkind to me, weak is not what you are going to remember about me," said Al Capone.

I have said that too. Not ever out loud. Not quite as cool, and only when I can remember the quote. But still.

Another woman walked by me soon afterward and smiled. She said with no judgment or deceit in her voice, "I love the idea of writing a grocery store name in the checkbook register. How clever."

We both smiled. She winked. I knew right then I had met a new friend.

"We can only be friends if you are kind of snarky. Not full-on snarky, because that's no fun. And if you are not snarky at all, that won't work either. If you are halfway snarky, then you are my kind of people." (Adapted from Someecards.)

If we are being honest, this quote sums up friendships quite nicely [insert wink].

Stay Connected

If a friend or the friend's close family member is going through a significant medical procedure, call or text before and after the procedure. Let your friend know you are thinking of her. Be ready to talk if she calls. Go over and sit with her if she asks. Bring food if she can eat or if she asks you to bring some food.

Or, the best part of this code, throw it all to hell and just show up. Bring bacon, chocolate, and wine (or bourbon) and hold her hand. Nothing else will be needed. Well, maybe some sparkly earrings. And a superhero cape with special powers. Just in case. Let her know she had the power all along. Be her Glinda the Good Witch. Because everyone needs a few Glindas in her life.

Staying connected can be tough. We are busy, and we don't always make the time to connect with friends. Likewise, with all of the technology available, it is hard to know the best way to connect. I have some friends where our primary way of communicating is via texting or Facebook, while with others it is necessary to make an old-fashioned phone call or handwritten letter. No matter, it is always about stay-ing connected regardless of the way.

At one of the women's gatherings, a woman spoke of friendships and having some regrets over ones that were lost. She made the comment, "If a relationship is important, you have to invest in it. It doesn't just exist by itself."

We need to make deposits in order to get our returns.

Friendships often take on stronger meaning as we age. Many women speak of how the closest people in their lives are their women friends. Many family members and loved ones have passed on, and friendships become their family. They are all that is left.

Another woman shared when asked about her friend-ships, "I never thought I would be alone at this age. I always thought my ex-husband and I would grow old together play-ing with our grandchildren. It brought me great sadness. I have since discovered the strongest relationship I have is with these women here tonight. I know I can pick up the phone, and I am not alone anymore. They fill me up."

So keep this code sacred. Stay connected to those who give meaning, joy, and purpose to your life. Stay connected to those who fill you up simply by showing up. Let go of the ones who drain you. Life is too short to run on empty.

Anticipate

While this code may not seem as obvious as the others, it

holds quite a bit of value. This is the one where your friends know you so well that they know how to anticipate what you may need or may need to do. Anticipating comes from the familiarity of being together and having shared many things between you. It is also about how one person can sense, without even being told, what the situation is calling for. Anticipating calls on a person's intuition and their ability to act on it.

To anticipate is to know that if this isn't said or done now (fill in the blank), this (fill in the blank) may happen. For example, a friend following this code will know to tell you when there is food in your teeth, anticipating an embarrassing feeling when you look in the mirror later and wonder how many people saw that piece of spinach. Or they will give you the universal sign for: "You have something on your face" by gesturing a hand movement across their cheek or whatever area is affected, looking at the spot directly, and making a wiping movement. Or they may say out loud: "Do this (making a sweeping hand gesture). There is something on your face."

This is also demonstrated by a friend giving you a tissue when your nose begins to dribble and you seem unaware (why does that happen anyhow?), but everyone else is noticing. Or by offering you a piece of gum after your taco salad. Enough said there.

All of these things are in anticipation of what could happen if not addressed. And it is a very good friend that can do these things without stepping out of any rhythm going on at the time. Effortlessly. Flawlessly.

Among the already-mentioned examples, there is the anticipation offered by a good friend who knows what you need to hear at just the right moment. She knows when a hug will do just as much as words. Or when it is time to sit in silence. Having a friend who knows the Anticipation Girlfriend Code is priceless. She is kind, thoughtful, and just simply knows. She knows you. She knows the importance of the friendship, and she knows just what to do to keep it important.

Girl friendship codes are a sustaining life force to any friendship. The codes help set the parameters around expectations and bring clarity to what is needed to sustain the friendship. By having codes, we learn what we can disagree on and what to stay away from. We learn what needs to be supported and what needs to be dismissed. None are written in stone and, in fact, codes can change with each friendship. Friendship codes have been passed on from generation to generation, friend to friend, and have stood the test of time. Do we really want to mess with something that started from, "Do onto others . . ."?

Ninjas Unite

Women need friends. We need old memories shared and new memories made. We especially need real friendships.

As we grow older it becomes less important to have many friends. We just need the ones that have meaning and purpose for us.

In one of the women's gatherings, I was especially moved by the women who attended. All were in their sixties and have been friends for many years, some since they were in school. Their love and absolute solidarity for each other was so strong it could be felt. Their friendship saturated the room. What moved me so deeply were the stories they shared, always describing an event, what they learned from it, and how one, a couple, or all of the women in the room had been there for that story. To not have one or more of their friends experience a life event with them would mean the event would have been rewritten; their life story would have been re-recorded.

Kathy put their friendship in great perspective when she said, "As a group of friends we live like every day is a gift. We do not take anything for granted, including our friendships. We take turns lifting each other up when we need it, and we tell each other the truth when we need it."

I need good friends to discuss things with. I am now at that age where conversations with good friends typically include discussing body ailments. I used to think this was something "older" people spoke about. Now that I am older, I speak of it.

I have talked ad nauseum with good friends about which products really do help with elimination and keep you regular. I have detailed conversations with friends at lunch, yes while eating, about my entire colonoscopy procedure, including prep (which was awful), during the exam (I liked this part due to the drugs used and the warm blanket), and after the exam (passing gas in a recovery room with only a curtain between people).

Now these are good friends!

I have friends who talk openly of their own and/or their spouses' memory loss, and all the worries and embarrassment that accompany that. I have listened as friends share the deep, deep angst of losing a loved one to Alzheimer's. As a friend, I know that the best I can do is listen. No fancy words or stories. Just simply do nothing and listen. I view this act as a pure privilege. What a gift I have been given to be the person someone trusts so much with some of her most personal of stories. It is grace filled.

My friends and I have talked of our own mortality. Our worries for this lump or that spot. We have talked about how our bodies do not feel as young as our minds do, how in our aging mind we are still quite physical and in shape. And then we go outside for a walk, and our asthma kicks in or our knee gives out within minutes.

Yes, aging gives us much to talk about. But the truth is, in spite of how our body is working, we can continue to do those things that bring us pleasure. Just because we reach a certain age, we do not have to allow ourselves to give up or give in.

In reflecting on my own aging and the changes I have experienced, I have learned a few things along the way. One very important lesson I know is I have to have friends. I need friends. We all need friends. I need the knots in the rope lifeline.

From the book *This Chair Rocks: A Manifesto Against Ageism* by Ashton Applewhite,[2] New York columnist Anne C. Roark, of *New Old Age* blog, writes, "In a strange twist of fortune—some might call poetic justice—age can bring with it something of a reversal in gender roles. The rise of an old girls' network, friends and family who see women through a lifetime of transitions, often contrasts sharply with the decline of the professional associations that secure young men's places in the world but offer little support or solace later in life." Further evidence of girl power . . . to which I say, "*Duh!*"

Many of us are lucky enough to have certain moments come to mind when we think of using the lifeline rope. My wish for all of us is that, as we age, we have many lifeline moments come to mind. One particular time for me was when my husband and I signed the paperwork for our new home. We had a couple of days before we were scheduled to move in. On the evening before the move-in day, my best "all the time" friend, Judy, came over to see where we would be living. All I had in the house were two lawn chairs, a

2 *This Chair Rocks: A Manifesto Against Ageism* by Ashton Applewhite, Networked Books, 2016.

flashlight, plastic cups, napkins, cleaning products, and toilet tissue. Being the good friend she was, she brought the wine.

After our tour of the house, we decided to open the bottle of wine. We set up the two lawn chairs, grabbed a lovely set of plastic cups, and began to look through the picture glass window at the beautiful backdrop of trees, wildlife, and sunset. We clinked our glasses, said a toast, and simply sat there. By simply sitting there, I knew my friend understood that moving to this house was hard and a little bit sad for me. It meant a big change for our family. I knew in her silence she wanted to give me the time to be present in this space and take it all in before all of the hustle and bustle occurred and before others took its space. This silence, this peace, was her gift to me.

She made mention only a few times about how wonderful this view will be to look at each night. She talked only once of how beautiful the sunsets will be and of how lucky I was to be able to hear the owls say their good-night. And when it was time to go because the sun had set, she simply looked over and asked if I was ready. I knew she wasn't just asking if I was ready to leave that night. It was the question I needed to answer for myself about beginning this new journey in my life. I was scared and unsure, but, yes, I was ready.

As I think of my friends over the years, I am reminded of how blessed I have been in my life with various women. There are times when no words are needed, no reason to discuss great world problems. There is a special, unspoken language that occurs between two people who are truly meant to be friends. Some pass through our life and their only imprint is to have been there for a moment in time. But that moment was an important one. They leave their mark exactly where it needs to be at just the right time. They are the angels who fly in and out of our lives. They whisper their words of wisdom to us and seem to know just what to say. Those are the friends whose arrival we can never anticipate, but we know they find their way to us. Every time. Just in time.

Still, there are others who come into our lives, and they never leave. They are our "all the time" friends. They give us just what we need when we need it, whether we think we need it or not! Those are the friends who will never let us walk out of the bathroom at our child's wedding with tissue stuck to the back of our dress, especially if the dress is tucked into our large underpants. Those are the friends we keep for life. They arrive in third grade and never leave our side through high school and boyfriends, multiple shades of eye shadow, and hairstyles. They are the ones sharing their hair spray and perfume. They walk down the aisle at our wedding, holding our heart before we give it away, knowing we have never been more excited or more afraid in our whole lives. They are the friends who hold our firstborn and the others to come. They hold our hand as we worry and celebrate every little or big, every this or that. They are there for the tears, laughter, and fears. They watch as our children grow older and our eyes grow tired. These all-the-time friends were there when a parent died or a loved one slipped away. They carried our pain so we could find rest. These are the friends who understand that when we are about to act crazy, we still want to look cute. Yes, these are the friends who know us the best. They are the reason we even know about the knots in the lifeline rope. The knots are strategically placed so we both know where to pull in just the right spots. I am reminded of a quote from E.B. White, "I arise in the morning torn between a desire to improve or save the world and a desire to enjoy or savor the world. This makes it hard to plan the day."

A good friend will excitedly say, "Do whatever makes you happiest today!"

Aging can bring about great reflection. When I reflect about my friendships, I am struck at the intuitiveness women have when being good friends. At times no words are spoken. Nothing but knowing. We each gather up what the other drops. We take the broken pieces and put together a most beautiful mosaic and give it back. We teach each other how to appreciate the simple act of kindness. A card in the mail, a text that says we are being thought of, an impromptu invite for a glass of wine at a local outdoor café. The list can go on and on. It is simple. We are friends, and that will be enough.

We all want friends who mean the world to us. The kind

of friends we would do anything for. And if need be, we would say to them:

"If ninjas captured you, I would spend all of my free time training to be a ninja, which might take some time, since I am very far from being that. But I want you to know I would eventually save you." —Logan Rhoades

In gratitude for knowing a friend is a wonderful thing to have, and a friend is a wonderful thing to be.

CHAPTER 4

Love Through the Lens of Gratitude

*"And I'd choose you; in a hundred lifetimes;
in a hundred worlds; in any version of
reality; I'd find you and I'd choose you."*
—The Chaos of Stars

I WILL NEVER HAVE to ask if I am loved. I know I am. It is something that brings me peace and joy each day. I have learned that being loved by even one person brings me to a sweet and wonderful place.

As of this writing, I have been married thirty-one years. I should also mention this has been to the same man. Knowing the exact number of years I have been married is important, as I seem to either add or subtract a year when someone asks me. I have a hard time remembering the year we were married and then subtracting that year from the current year to come up with the total number of years married. It's hard math. So suffice it to say, I have been married for a good number of years. What I really don't seem to understand is how all of this time has gone by. Where did it go? And because my math is so bad, I have decided it really isn't about the years; it is about the experiences we've had together. That's what I remember. Not the math, but the love.

As I write this chapter, I am very aware of the fact that my husband will be reading this. I want to make sure, God willing, we have thirty-one more years together! So I hope when he reads this, he understands why I just had to write down a few of these things in order to offer kinship to other aging couples. Plus some of these stories are just plain funny!

I think I speak for many older couples that have been married for a good long time when I say it isn't always easy. I can say this because I have a great marriage. But we have worked at it. Our marriage now is nothing like it was when we first married. For that I am grateful. Not because it was awful in the beginning, it was just different compared to now. Our marriage today suits me better.

Now I see my husband as the person who makes our love story the one I want to be in—a story where happily ever after doesn't mean it is not without its bumps, twists, and turns along the way. I no longer see my relationship with my husband as perfect; rather, it is perfectly playing itself out. This took me a minute or two to figure out.

I lived many years thinking that in order to have a great

love affair, everything had to fall into place. When something in our marriage did not, I tended to see it as a flaw, something that needed repair. Now I see when things do not go the way I think they should (which really they should), it isn't because something turned out wrong, but because it turned out differently. Mostly it is different than how I anticipated it would be. Earlier, my Happily Ever After lived in my head filled with fantasy. When real life didn't match up, then obviously something was wrong. Now I know that being in a relationship is about give and take. Some days are better than others and this too shall pass.

Now I know my Happily Ever After is after I get mad about not turning out the lights, or after starting a project and not finishing it, or not really even needing to start it in the first place, or after we discuss paying the bills. Because in the big picture, this stuff doesn't really matter. In fact, some of those things I argued about were really a precursor to what was really bugging me. Now I know to say what I need and I skip the minutiae. The truth is, after all these years, I am still deeply and madly in love with my husband. How great is that?

When interviewing women, some of the most detailed conversations occurred around being in a relationship. Many of the women had been with their partners for many years, and some were divorced or widowed. A common thread of conversation from women still with their partners was either around not needing as much time together now that they were older, or feeling trapped into spending even more time together. For many couples, they were either experiencing retirement or receiving disability benefits due to health concerns. With that, the dynamics of their relationships changed.

Many women, such as Maureen, age sixty-five, talked of having to adjust to being with each other more. "Now that the kids are gone and they have their own life, and I do not have to report to anyone in a work environment, I want to manage my own time and do my own thing. Sometimes my own thing has nothing to do with my husband (also retired)." She added, "My husband is content to sit around and read. Not me. I want to take classes, travel, and drink lots of wine with my girlfriends!"

She became reflective for a moment and added, "I love my husband. We just have to figure this whole time together thing out."

I suspect she is not alone.

Likewise, many women reported that travel was one of the best ways to spend time together with a partner. Now that their family was grown and more independent, they were able to spend their money and their time doing things that had meaning and purpose for them. They could share in doing something together as well as explore on their own if need be.

In addition to finding more time together, there were many conversations around finding new love with each other as well. It seemed from many of the women interviewed having someone special in our life becomes even more important as we grow older. As our family structure changes, having consistency with one person becomes a treasure.

When that treasure is at risk for being lost, it puts things into perspective as shared by a woman I met named Kim, age sixty-one. She talked about how when her husband went through brain cancer, it put everything into perspective for her, including her love for her husband, their marriage, and the faith they lived by. She was struck by how many people were there to help her and her husband get through this very trying time. What stood out is how her husband became her hero. She realized that she was busy doing many more things for him at the time he was going through all of his treatments and surgeries, but still she found herself seeing who he was again through his determination to get better and fight through the cancer.

In the end it was her husband who brought her peace, not the other way around. That was her perception. And in the end the experience brought them closer. Having gone through a time when she wondered if he was going to make it, her priorities became clearer. She found herself understanding how fragile life is and that each day is truly a gift to treasure as best you can.

As I listened to Kim share this story, I was struck at how her words were carefully chosen. It was clear to me that she had been introspective with all that she went through with her husband and his cancer. It was clear to me that she had been changed. However, what was most clear was how she felt such a strong love for her husband when he was sick and how she continues to feel pure love and admiration for him now. Her love continues to grow stronger. Listening to her, I am reminded of the fragility of life and of love as well.

When I spoke to women about their partners in life, many had funny stories to share, and many of the stories were about sex. Not really a surprise there. Happily, several women shared that sex was even more enjoyable now that the children were out of the home. "No more having to time when to go at it," said Sharon. "As soon as the kids left the house, when they lived at home with us, and we had at least twenty minutes, and we hadn't eaten anything to produce gas, AND we both had energy left in us, bam, off to the bedroom we would go! Now we do not have to run into the bedroom. We walk into the bedroom or shout out to the other person to see if they are interested or not. "

Sharon added after thinking about it, "I think I just made our sex life sound more boring now then when we had kids! I think maybe we should start running into the bedroom again!"

Given the number of women I interviewed, I was always looking for something to stand out. Something that would give me great insight into women and aging, and for this chapter on relationships and love, I had one such woman. Her name was Barbara Lee, age sixty-five. When discussing relationships she said, "I must put in a good plug for being a lesbian. I have been in relationships where intimacy is so important. I feel real lucky to have experienced that. It is so different than two men in a relationship. In my opinion, that relationship seems to be centered around sexual activity and less intimacy. Heterosexual relationships seem to be about always balancing between intimacy and non-intimate experiences. Making compromises like that would wear me out. Lesbian relationships are all about intimacy. I am currently not in a relationship, but I am a friend with every single woman I have dated. That is how close we became and are still becoming."

Her wonderful words helped me realize I still have so much to learn about relationships, and that my norm isn't everybody else's norm. Mostly I learned a great lesson about the importance of having someone you want to be your best self around. And when you are not, the person is still there.

As I interviewed women about relationships, I noticed that talking about sex was a little uncomfortable. I had women, such as Linda, age sixty-two, shout out, "We're having the best sex we have ever had!" all the way to Rita, age sixty-two, asking, "Now, what is a sex drive again?"

The whole topic of sex as it related to aging was worthy of great discussion because there were so many different answers given.

**Note to my grown children: Okay, this is a really great section of the book for you NOT to read. Honestly, I know you too well, and this will seem embarrassing to you. And I get it. So move along to the next section. Please. Just listen to your mother!

I find that being married this long, as well as being this age, also provides a pass for a few things. By "pass" I mean, things are understood and accepted. Like sex. Having a pass is a way of understanding we no longer come to bed wearing many suggestive or sexy items. In fact, some of the items we now wear are downright completely opposite of suggestive or sexy. Though some of the items worn to bed still offer suggestions, they consist mostly of suggesting, "This is the night, possibly like last night, that I really just want to go to sleep." These aforementioned items can also include going to bed wearing mouth guards, CPAP masks and hoses attached to a machine. And possibly earplugs.

My husband and I, we are quite the pair. On any given night we look and sound like we are ready to take flight or be in a fight. My mouth guard definitely works as a protector to my teeth as I am quite the teeth grinder when I sleep. Side note: I need a new one, but my insurance will not allow me to have a new one. (Don't get me started on the whole other topic for aging: healthcare.) The material used in mouth guards is supposed to be indestructible . . . well, I am missing almost an entire side from grinding while wearing it! The mouth guard inserted also sends a signal of "This is not a good night for sex." A quick tap on my guard followed by a slurry-worded "I have my mawf guar in" is usually enough information needed. This is followed by a hard-to-understand response from my husband, "No worries, I have my CPAP on."

I can't help but think he sounds very similar to Darth Vader. Trust me, Darth Vader is not even on my list of people to be romantic with. Not that I have a list.

So we have a routine. We know we are okay. No need to ask, "Is everything alright?" because we are choosing sleep over sex. Because we REALLY are choosing sleep over sex.

Sex when you are aging is still wonderful, intimate, and a beautiful way of sharing your love for one another. But I would be remiss if I did not include it is also becoming more of a challenge and, on occasions, it can be funny. Our bodies are changing. With those changes comes some oopsies. By oopsies I mean, "Oopsie, I should probably go to the bathroom. I'll be right back," or "Oopsie, sounds like I am still digesting dinner." And, "Oopsie, we need to stop. I have a leg cramp!"

With aging, we may experience other maladies that can interfere with being sexual and intimate. Some of the women I interviewed shared that as their bodies changed the way they are sexual has changed. Marlys, age seventy-one, gave great insight into what changes might take place. She stated, "While I am no longer able to enjoy sex in the vigorous way

I had when I was younger, I am still a sexual being. I enjoy the pleasures experienced as my husband and I continue to be intimate. However, sex is no longer based on the ending. It is now based on having the desire to even start!"

Other women shared changes experienced in their bodies that made being intimate more difficult or even uncomfortable. Medications that caused vaginal dryness, digestive issues, fatigue, or even ones that take away the desire were discussed as big changes for women as they age. This, on top of medications men take that cause impotence, lack of desire, or even medications that counteract impotence, can affect being intimate.

As Marlys added, "There is nothing like waiting for a pill to kick in to be intimate. It's like waiting for the turkey built-in timer to pop out. You keep checking to see if things are ready. And if you are still awake or interested, then things can finally get going. All I can say is, you better have a good sense of humor as you age!"

It should be noted that medical or mental health conditions or physical disabilities are not laughing matters. Having a condition that already creates hardships will obviously add to the complexity of being a sexual being. Many of us experience physical changes as we age that may hinder our ability to be physical in the way we used to be. Understanding how to be creative and unapologetic is critical to having wonderful intimate experiences. And as Marlys pointed out, having a good sense of humor doesn't hurt either.

As you can imagine, many women in the interviews gig-gled their way through our conversations around sex. In one of the women gatherings, Rita, age fifty-four, shared that it wasn't that she didn't want to have sex, it was just that by the time she got to bed she was so tired. Her body would not respond the way she wanted it to. So sometimes she had sex just for her husband. She also admitted to watching a little TV during what she called "the festivities." Her whole point to this story was that she still wanted to be there for her hus-band. She cared about what he wanted and felt bad that she wasn't always able to be in the same place as he was with regard to desiring sex. This started a conversation with the other women attending this particular gathering about hor-mone replacement. I think by the end, Rita realized there was hope. I think she also realized others watched a little TV during the festivities as well!

The good news is if you know someone well enough and long enough, when any issues occur, and they will occur, they typically are nonissues. Sure they may call for giggles and laughs. But what better way to have intimacy than to be so comfortable with someone that no matter what happens, you are still in this together and the relationship still grows stronger. Having sex, as you grow older, happens. Contrary to what some might think, it can remain a very important part of a relationship for a very long time. It's all about man-aging the oopsies, mouth guards, CPAPS and all!

As Mark Twain said, "Age is an issue of mind over matter. If you don't mind, it doesn't matter."

Having sex is not the only one way to share intimacy. The other parts to intimacy, I would never want to turn down. The touch of a hand, the smile given, the look of knowing, the words of understanding, and the words "I love you" spoken without any reason. Those are the intimate moments shared between my husband and me when I will never say, "I have my mawf guard in."

Then There Were Five

Out of my husband's and my love came three wonderful children. Now they are no longer children. They are on their way in age and careers. They no longer require rides to any practices or school or anywhere else, for that matter. They live in their own places, and they pay their own bills (well, they pay most of their own bills and live mostly in their own places). Besides my husband, they are the loves of my life. But to me they will always be my children. The question becomes: What do I call them now? Kids? Children? Adult-children? Really, what do I call them?

The answer may lie in the backstory. To describe the love I have for my children, and from so many other women I speak to about this, is to speak of it in layers. There is the overall layer of "I love you to pieces!" It is the kind of love that happens when no words are spoken. All that is needed is to hear their names, think of each face, and bring a memory to mind, and my heart explodes with a deep-seated love. It is powerful beyond words. It is beyond. There are the other layers of love that come in stages and are unique for each child, the layers of love from the absolute joy and pride that happen as they accomplish the small and not-so-small tasks of life. The layers of love also come from hopes, dreams, and goals as I watch them experience each stage of their lives. The layers come from worry, pain, and fear as I see them stumble and falter. All of the layers entwine and make a specially designed, invisible cloak suitable for each individual child of mine.

As a mom, I want to take this cloak, wrap it around them, and protect them no matter how old they are. I want to wrap the cloak around them to feel the power of my love. Not just for one moment, but for all the moments to come. I don't think this deep love and desire to protect them will ever leave me. Nor would I want it to. They are my children and they always will be.

In a gathering of women being interviewed, Karen shared, "I know that my children do not need me like they used to. I actually like the freedom this brings me. But I still want to feel important in their life. I try to stay out of things unless asked, but that doesn't mean I don't have opinions about what they're doing! I share those with my girlfriends now!"

This comment was met with an almost audible, "Amen, sister!"

Many of the women talked about how hard it is to stay out of their children's lives if they think their children are making mistakes, and they still want to save them from having to experience any hardships. Many heads were bobbing and words of "For sure" and "Absolutely" were shared throughout this particular conversation.

In another women's gathering Lisa, age fifty-five, shared her perspective on having adult children and how she makes it work. "I know I have created a dependence between me and my daughters," Lisa said, "but I'm okay with it. I like talking to them almost daily and being a part of their lives."

She became reflective and went on to say, "When I had cancer, it became pretty clear to me what was important and who I was going to live for. It was my immediate family. My daughters and my husband. They mean everything to me. Sometimes I think I should back off with my daughters, and I know my husband thinks I should, but I find I really do like to be a part of their world. I don't think I could give that up no matter how old I get."

I believe Lisa's sharing brings us to a place of understanding the common thread we share as aging women with children. We still want to have strong, close relationships with our children, and we will figure out how to do this (hopefully) in the way that works best for each of us.

For me, I always knew I wanted to be a mom. I believed that it was a part of my destiny from early on. This may have come from my innate sense of caretaking. I was also blessed to have wonderful extended family members, such as my great-grandmother, affectionately called Grandma Graham. She was the epitome of what I thought having a family should be. I always felt blessed and cared for in her presence. I grew up in a divorced family when divorce was not really happening in too many families around me. While I fretted about having parents not together, I found solace in my time spent with Grandma Graham. Since I did not have an intact family growing up, I would dream about having one. So out of what I saw as brokenness, came wholeness.

Luckily for me I found a great partner to have my family with. Interestingly, neither one of us came from the perceived perfect, 2.5-children, white-picket-fence family. His father passed away when he was three years old. He had four siblings and a wonderful mom who had to work to support her children. So my husband and I learned together. And that is what made us perfect.

Having children is a gift. One that I will never take for granted. I know others who do not have their own children and have great sadness around that. So for me to want and then receive children, I feel lucky. I feel blessed.

I also know others who have chosen not to have children, and I commend them for knowing. Linda, age sixty, at one of the gatherings shared, "Deb is sixty-two and she is the coolest person our kids know," gesturing to include everyone in the room and looking directly at Deb. "Even though you never had any children of your own, you always made sure to include our kids in everything. They love you. I love you. I want to acknowledge the difference you made in our lives and in our family's lives."

Hard to take notes when there are tears in my eyes.

Now with my own children well on their way in adulthood, I still have questions I want to ask them such as, "How did I do? Did you have a good childhood? Are there things I could have done differently? What role do you want me to play now that we are all getting older?"

I mentioned this to a friend of mine who suggested I ask them, not her.

Good point. Fine.

A woman named Beth, age forty-nine, shared a sentiment eloquently about having children and how she hoped they knew how great she thought they were. She shared through her tears, "Sometimes I get so mad at both my husband and my kids, I could scream. But what I have been trying to do is come from a place of love, so they know that is more important than anything else that has happened. I want them to know I love them first and foremost through anything that happens."

It was clearly a moving testament to her love and devotion to her kids to do those things that brought out the best in them. I don't know any mom, younger or older, that would disagree.

I know I cannot keep my children in my home and keep everything the same. Nor would I want to. I just don't want them to forget about me. I want a text every now and again. Maybe even a "like" on my Facebook page. I want to know I am still important in their lives.

The question of what role I should play now that my children are getting older gives me hope. It gives me hope because it means we are still in each other's lives. Now that my children are grown, I really do want to know what they would like from me.

When they were younger I knew how to tell them what to do, how to listen, come up with ideas, and give them chores to complete. I want to know what they would like from me now. What I don't know is how to take off that cloak of layers I talked about earlier. I don't think I can. I still want to drape it around them for love, safety, and protection. For now and perhaps until the end, I hope they don't mind wearing that extra piece of clothing. All day. Every day.

This Is the Frosting on the Cake of Life!

"Gush" is the only word I can think of to fully describe what women act like about having grandchildren. I have never in my life met so many women who are head over heels, absolutely in love, and would do anything for their grandchildren! Any mention of grandchildren, for those who have them, and a love fest ensues. It is beautiful and moving every time. It never gets old for me to see women beam.

I have not been fortunate enough to have grandchildren yet, so I am relying solely on my interviews with women who do. Let me tell you the Grandmas, Nanas, GiGis, and Maw-Maws had plenty to say.

I learned about how important grandchildren are when I asked this question, "What makes you most happy?"

Women lit up and almost immediately said, "My grandchildren."

I had one woman immediately pull out photos of her grandchildren as if just saying the word "grandchildren" triggers an automatic response and ritual. Part of the ritual included being updated with the new pictures sent by the parents of the grandchildren. Suddenly those parents, her own children, no longer had names. After fifteen minutes of excitement and gushing, I politely asked if we could look at the photos after the interviews were complete. I was smiling when I asked, but I don't think anyone else was after I asked.

Message received . . . don't interrupt the sharing of grandchildren pictures.

Julie began talking about the renewed joy she felt for the simplest things. "When I am with my grandchildren I get to see life through their eyes. It keeps me young and wanting to do things. Just going to the zoo and looking at all the animals is so exciting for them. Then I get excited. Honestly these grandchildren bring me such happiness."

Karen quickly jumped in with, "And they get to go home!"

All agreed in a way that seemed heartfelt and understood.

At one particular gathering, Ann Marie, age sixty, shared that she had lost a grandchild. She went on to talk of the devastating pain she experienced: "I always believed there was an order to things. Older people die first. When my grandson died it was as if everything turned upside down. There wasn't any order."

Hearing Ann Marie and seeing her eyes, I felt I was given a glimpse of that gut-wrenching sense of love and then loss you wish on no one ever. For a brief time my life intersected with hers, and I felt this deep pain and sadness. She had to move on while someone much younger would never get that chance.

Words escape me.

Not surprisingly, many women shared that their role with their grandchildren is very different than what it was with their own children. However, women also shared about the new added worries they feel. Now they had new people to worry about, and they wanted to know how to balance the role they play. All reminisced about not liking it when their parents offered advice on their parenting styles. Now the tables were turned. The jury is out on the exact way to do this.

Without a doubt, I can say with utmost surety, being a grandparent is one of the best things in life. It is the frosting on the cake of life!

My Mother, Myself
(or Something Like That)

There is another kind of love that develops differently as we age. It is the love for our aging parents. If you are lucky enough to have parents still alive, you can certainly appreciate how different the relationship is with them as we age and as they age. It seems to me that in a blink of an eye my parents got old. I don't mean that in any negative way. As a matter of fact, my mother is still alive and just spent an entire week up at the cabin and recently "liked" my new post on Facebook. She is definitely aging, but she is also keeping some kick in her step as best she can. I also know she is having her struggles as part of aging. I find myself wanting to help but not wanting to push. It is a delicate balance of switching roles—much like being on a tightrope with someone and passing each other on the same rope, in mid-air and not wanting to knock yourself or the other person down.

For those of us with aging parents now or in our past, we realize the roles change. I don't remember exactly when it happened for me. What I do know is that when my dad was ill, and especially in his last stage of life, I felt a switch happen. I became more of the parent and made more of the decisions as he became unable to. I fell into it naturally, but I could not shake the strange feeling about parenting my dad.

A fine line occurs when your parents need you to take care of them. By taking care of them, I do not mean to simply bring over some food or pick up something at the store. I mean really care for them. Feeding, bathing, getting them dressed, changing them, transporting them, etc. All that stuff we didn't think about doing for our parents until we have to. It takes some getting used to.

I found that when I began to take on this role, not only did my role change, but my love for them changed as well. It became enriched in a way that allowed me to feel a stronger bond with them. I began to have a better understanding of how they are as human beings. And I became more aware of them as spirit. I could sense them trying to just get by or in need of a little help in continuing to make their mark in this world. It is a humbling experience for me and, I imagine, for my parents as well.

I also think there is room for honesty when talking about becoming the parent to your parent(s). Simply stated, it is tough. I have interviewed many women, and one of the themes that has often emerged around aging parents is how hard it was/is to balance taking care of your immediate family as well as your parents in their times of need.

A friend of mine, Susan, age sixty-two, reported that her calendar was a mix of weekly medical appointments, including her own children, parents, and husband; work meetings; "take your pill" reminders; "time to bathe" reminders; dog grooming appointments; and a variety of other "things to do." What became painfully obvious is she had not one personal appointment for herself on the calendar.

This, she shared, was noted by the length of her unplucked and unwaxed eyebrows, the wispiness at the bottom of her hair dying for a cut, and the two-toned, unwelcomed hair color she saw in the mirror each day. She observed what most women do who take care of many people and things is permit the breakdown of caring for themselves.

I learned from personal experience that being a primary caregiver takes its toll. Not only on the caregiver, but also on the person needing the care. Having aging parents often removes them from being on our own list of who we can call for help. There is a sense of loss for us as the children, as well as a sense of loss for our parents. They know they cannot help as they used to and it can be hard to accept. It is not a comfortable place to be.

At one of the women's gatherings Chelle, age forty-nine, shared that she has a fear of losing both of her parents. She has not experienced any great loss in her life, and it worries her thinking what it will be like. She had a great insight to offer us about this. She said, "So I want to celebrate the time now. Celebrate now and not worry about the loss to come. It will get here soon enough."

Great advice for all of us for so many things.

Kim, age sixty-one, shared that she had buried her parents within six months of each other. She talked of being so immersed in the role of caregiver that it is still hard to shake off knowing what to do with her time. The deaths of both parents took a toll on her. It was obvious she was still strongly affected by the loss. Who wouldn't be? Among the things that helped her through the losses were her strong female friendships. Kim shared with the very group of strong friends at one of the women's gatherings, "I feel sadness for others who don't have what we have. You helped me to not stay in the mourning phase. I would have missed all that was to come. We live like every day is a gift and that helps us hold each other up."

Nothing like the love of good girlfriends.

Jan, age sixty, shared, "The loss of my parents put things into perspective for me. It's scary. I wonder if I will have any regrets? Like that I didn't do Facebook? I don't know. It's hard to lose both parents. That means I am getting closer to being next."

From personal experience when I was a caregiver for my dad, I can say that his not being able to help others, much less himself, was one of the hardest things to face. Like all of us, he wanted a purpose. When his body did not cooperate anymore, it was another reminder of time becoming more and more precious and of things he could not do. I remember feeling bad not asking my dad for help. I kept some things, like a kitchen project, from him. It seemed unkind to talk to him about it and not have him over to help, as he would have liked to. Or had in the past.

Jodi, age fifty-two, shared this about caring for her mom as she weathered having cancer, "I turned into the parent and that was hard to see and experience for all of us. It created a great sadness. Now, as I look at my parents, I know how lucky I am to have them around. But still they are not the same parents. They are not the same people they used to be."

It's true. We will all become "not the same people we used to be." If we are lucky enough to have the gift of time.

Jodi's story and others that were similar reminded me of a quote from Walt Whitman, "These are the days that must happen to you. You shall scatter with a lavish hand all that you learn or achieve. And those who love you shall rise to your example and be inspired."

With my own aging parents, I learned how to talk differently to them as they became different. Leaving out certain pieces of information or not talking about something too soon for fear the memory would not be as sharp. Something I would abhor if my kids did to me, but maybe will have a little bit of understanding, should it occur. I learned quickly how to navigate the waters of my parents aging as well as my own aging. And sometimes something's gotta give.

In keeping with honesty, sometimes caring for aging parents is frustrating. They may become too needy or dependent on you for some of the tasks you wish they could just do for themselves. I find this feeling wanes and waxes as I either get more sleep or don't. I am tired, too. I also worry that what I see in them will happen to me. Thus I have a rather large print "word find" book in my nightstand. To make sure I am still able to remember words and then find them. I try to practice my word searches regularly. And I play solitaire. And Candy Crush. If I remember.

As I am getting older, my body and mind like their sleep. The former also responds much better when its bangs have been trimmed and eyebrows waxed. To speak of being frustrated when caregiving for others and not of ourselves sounds selfish and unloving, but really, it could not be further from the truth. I get frustrated, AND I love my parents. I want to proclaim to all who care for their aging parents that this is okay. Feeling both is okay.

When we take the lens of gratitude and look through it when taking care of our parents, we can see another gift bestowed on us. No matter any of the history between you, a really cool thing happens when you allow yourself the opportunity to give of yourself, especially to your own parent.

I have heard of many love stories that include a child putting behind them all of the hurt, frustration, and anger to just be there for an ailing or aging parent. No strings attached. Those who have done this speak of feeling free to express their love for a parent for the first time. They wanted to be there to give what is needed and to be able to do so without the baggage, or at least not all of the baggage!

When there was an end, all spoke to wishing they had had more time. The adult-child caregivers missed being a part of their parent's journey, of their own journey with them, as their parent entered into and then left their last period of time on Earth. Everyone I talked to about this subject spoke of time and trying to make more of it as their parent journeyed to the end of their life.

A good reminder for us all, from Leo Christopher: "There is only one thing more precious than our time and that is who we spend it on."

Staying in gratitude provides a reality check that will guide decisions around what matters most and put things into perspective. Staying in gratitude brings love to the top. Every time.

You Should Have Known Me When I Was Younger!

I wasn't really sure what to say when a new friend said to me, "I wish you could have met my husband when he was younger. He was so energetic and able-bodied!"

I found her husband to be quite spry and able. It never crossed my mind to have met him at any other time in his life. But then I remembered: Sometimes I wish I were younger, too. Sometimes I don't want to be the age I am, either. Remembering that helped me understand why my friend might have said that.

What this also reminded me of is to love the ones you're with. I could see the love shine right out her beautiful eyes as she spoke of her husband as a more able-bodied man. The pride, the joy in sharing stories of him when he was younger, was solidly evident in her smile and storytelling hands. He was loved then and he is loved now.

The lesson revealed itself over and over from women I interviewed: "Love yourself for who you are now, not for what you used to be."

It's true.

As Sheila, age fifty-one, said, "There's an extra roll, thighs are a little bigger, but who cares? Aging is something not everyone is afforded. Love what you have now."

Truthfully, I struggle a little with the extra roll.

I also came to the conclusion that many of us might romanticize a little bit about what we looked like back in the day.

A common theme shared about what women love about aging is that the mind still thinks it is young, even if the body isn't. JoAnn, age sixty, shared that she forgets she can't do some things anymore, like sit on the floor. "I forget what I can and cannot do until I try and then I can't. In my mind I can do it all! Isn't that funny?"

Turns out the answer is: not at all. Many of us over fifty still think of ourselves as younger than we are.

Jodi, age fifty-two, summed it up nicely, "In our heads we believe we are a certain age. It's all about the perspective. When I am asked my age I answer forty, although I am fifty-two. Mostly because I can't remember my age and feel like I'm still forty!"

If I am being honest, sometimes I do wish I were younger. I don't want to go back into time or anything. I just want to be a different age in the time I am in now. I would probably pick early forties. I can see myself as perpetually being that age. Why? It was when I was my thinnest and had my best hair, eyesight, and ability to advance in my career. I remembered things, could multitask, and still thought of aging as in the future. My eyebrows were not thinning, except for the one long curly strand that still swirls around my eyeglasses, my hands did not need breaks from typing or holding a book or from lying in one position for too long, and my hips moved regularly without having to take ibuprofen.

When we were younger we didn't seem to be too caught up in the minutia that starts to happen as we age. Why would we be? We were in the midst of living a life filled with endless possibilities and capabilities. We were in love with love and life.

What can be gleaned from this? My takeaway is while my body may be going through a multitude of changes, my mind is still well intact. Becoming older is not an automatic sit-in-a-recliner-for-the-rest-of-our-days death sentence. Rather, it is a wonderful opportunity to have more intentional time to assess and determine what is important and what is not. For example, looking at all of the people and things I love through the lens of gratitude gives me peace of mind. I am grateful to have and had love in my life, and I am grateful for the experiences I have encountered. When I bring the belief of "What can I offer you?" and come from a place of love, like Beth spoke of, to everyone I meet for the first time or have loved forever, it ends up that MY cup runneth over every single time.

So this aging thing and love—talk about needing to strap on a seatbelt!

Aging changes, takes turns we didn't expect. It brings us down roads we didn't know existed and it challenges us to keep a good sense of direction and humor. And even after all of that, being loved and giving love becomes one of the greatest connectors for all of us no matter what our age.

I am reminded of my Grandma Graham again. She lived to be just shy of her 101st birthday. Even up to her last days, she told me how much she loved me and would hold out her age-weathered hand for me to hold. At the time, her hand looked so fragile to me that I worried about hurting her. If given the chance to hold her hand one more time, I would pray with her, hold it with both of my hands, and thank her for everything she gave to me, especially her unconditional love.

Jodi, age fifty-two, summed this all up very nicely by saying, "How can I be this age and not know this stuff? All of the white noise stops when I really pay attention to what is important. What I found out is love for another is what is really important. I don't want a catastrophe to happen before I remember this again!"

So let's pay attention. Let's not wait for something to happen to realize what is important . . . let's make it happen. As William Bradfield so eloquently says, *"There are those whose lives affect all others around them. Quietly touching one heart, who in turn, touches another. Reaching out to ends further than they would ever know."* There is no end time for letting someone know you love them. When I was younger I thought there was. I am glad I was wrong.

In gratitude for all who have touched my life and shown me love in ways I could have never known. In gratitude for the age I am now at this moment.

CHAPTER 5

Grief, Loss, and Being on the Wait List

"In the end only three things matter:
How much you loved, how gently you
lived, and how gracefully you let go of
things not meant for you."
—Buddha

I HAVE BEEN TO several funerals in the last couple of months. A few were called celebrations of life, and the person was cremated. A wonderful picture of them was on display as a way to remember them, which caused me to wonder: what picture would I have on display if I decided to have a celebration-of-life service? Questions rolled through my mind about what age I should be in the picture, how much of me should be in the picture, and which haircut was the best for me in pictures. A silly barrage of thoughts, but important to me nonetheless, and certainly something to consider. Other funerals I attended had an open casket. To be honest, I would have preferred a photo of the deceased. However, each are very acceptable end-of-life remembrances. Yet I am not committed to the way in which I would like to be remembered. Casket, urn, or sprinkled?

Trust me, as you may already know, this conversation isn't always a huge pick-me-up. Turns out there isn't always a great way to start a conversation with someone about end-of-life decisions. I used to be uncomfortable to be asked whether I was going to be cremated or buried. For some reason it seemed too personal, sort of like asking, "What kind of underpants do you wear?"

As I have matured, I am a little more comfortable talking about what to do with my body when I'm no longer in it. And I don't really care if people know I wear large underpants.

Given the choices between being buried or cremated, I will admit that I have some reservations about cremation. I have to remind myself that I will no longer be alive, so what difference does it make if I am cremated or not? It seems to be a cost-effective way to dispose of the dead, and yet I can't help feeling a little weird about it. I mean, shouldn't a person feel absolutely confident in a decision such as this? I have always assumed that everyone else is confident about the decisions about what to do with their body once dead. I'm not. So I started to ask more questions.

What better place to begin asking what others are deciding than while out to lunch with a friend, right? "Are you going to be cremated or buried?" I ask my girlfriend in a voice trying to sound like my next question will be if she went to any good movies lately.

"I think cremated. But why would you ask me that?" my friend asked while eating her salad with no onions or peppers, light on the dressing.

I haven't asked her, but based on her lunch, she (like me) probably can't tolerate certain foods. I immediately sympathized. On the other hand, she looked annoyed with my question. I take this as a signal to tread a little lighter.

After finishing my larger-than-necessary bite of a cheeseburger with nothing but pickles and ketchup on it, I said, "I thought you were for sure going to be cremated. You said so when I asked you this awhile back. I am asking again because I thought you would say yes again and then I would be more comfortable with cremation! To be honest, I need you to make up your mind, so I can make up my mind!"

I said this realizing how selfish this all sounds.

"Well, why did you ask again if I already told you?" asked my friend, who I think was feeling more defensive with each bite of salad, or maybe just mad about eating a salad. She continued, "Look, I am still ninety-nine percent sure I am going to be cremated, but not one hundred percent sure. Why is this even important to you?"

I had to think about that. Why *was* this so important to me? And really, was it any of my business about her desire, or anyone else's, to be cremated or not? I could sense her frustration with me. "I don't know," I answered. "I think it has to do with my own indecision. I figured if everybody else was settled on cremation, I could be, too. I want everybody else to decide for me by deciding for themselves, sort of like I do when ordering food off the menu. I never know what to order, so I wait until others order." I wanted to add "unless they order salads."

I could tell by her eyes that I was taking us to a place over lunch that wasn't really welcomed like the coffee was. But I really wanted to learn how other people decide what to do with their body once they die.

"So you're not sure?" I asked sheepishly, like a dog who had ripped a pillow apart and the owner had just come home. She looked down at her napkin and refolded it.

When she looked up she continued, "I am pretty sure I am going to be cremated. But I have some fears and doubts as well. I just think cremation is the way I am leaning."

"What if you get hit by a car on the way home today, God forbid [Am I supposed to do a sign of the cross here? I never know], and you die? Who knows your true wishes?"

Now I am on a roll. "What if your husband decides to have you buried and holds an open-casket viewing for you? Is that what you want? He knows you are leaning toward cremation, but what if he decides he didn't know for sure and decides to bury you instead?"

This roll I am on is going downhill faster and faster. I

probably should stop, and most people would, but I have this inane ability to keep going until I am sure I have made my point. In reflecting on this conversation, I realize the questions I was asking her were really about my own worries.

"Fine," my friend says. "If that is what my husband decides, then fine."

I was growing tense. "What about bugs getting into the casket once you are buried? Don't you worry about that? And the dirt? Do you worry about being underground in all that dirt? Or feeling claustrophobic? And . . ." No more coffee for me.

"Honestly, why do you even worry about this stuff?" asks the friend who was now clearly done with lunch.

She asked a great question, again.

It's true. I am worried. Death has never really been something I was comfortable with. Ever. I have vivid memories of family members' funerals. None elicit great feelings for me.

I have a few things I need to consider before making a final decision about whether to be buried or cremated. Part of this comes from the realization that I have already lived the majority of my life. I guess I feel like I have to make a decision now, before . . . you know.

If I am to be buried I will most likely have a designated time for a viewing. In my faith there is a custom for others to walk up to an open casket with the deceased inside. Having been to a few myself, I know the general idea of how this goes. My hands will be folded, looking very similar to my pose when I am alive after having nothing more to say, which, ironically when I die, will be true. My eyes will be closed, and I will resemble a figure similar to those found in Madame Tussaud's wax museum, only not an artistically crafted wax figure. People looking in at me will notice what I am wearing.

How do I know this? Because I do this at funerals.

Why is this a problem for me? For starters, I do not yet have a designated person to pick out my ensemble. Anyone could be responsible for what I wear. It is clear that I will need to leave some written instructions. I have a husband and a son who are color-blind and a daughter who has great fashion sense for herself, but we are twenty-nine years apart in age! My other son takes his sister out to help with his clothes shopping. So that leaves me with designating a friend to pick out my clothes or maybe write out my wishes in my end-of-life healthcare directive.

In the end, literally and figuratively, will it really matter what I wear? If I were to answer this question now, yes, it does matter to me. For now, I am leaning toward my favorite sweatpants and sweatshirt. That way I know I will be comfortable. They fit. And in the end, literally and figuratively, it is who I am. Casual, comfy, and fairly simple in things I like to wear.

Moving past the clothes decision leads me to the hair, makeup, and facial hair plucking. If I am to be viewed before burial, I will need someone who knows me to put on my makeup. I do not want a situation where I end up looking like I died while performing in a vaudeville act. I am a minimalist for makeup these days. What that means is I have several layers I put on to give me the minimalist look. There are a great number of powder containers in my left bathroom drawer. I use almost every one of them. Not every day. And I don't use the two containers way in the back. The point is, I need someone to know what I wear and where the makeup is so as not to have any comments made about my makeup and how different I look.

I know this is stupid, but I loathe going to wakes and hearing others comment on how well they look. "Doesn't she look natural?" or, "She looks so peaceful."

Really? Because the obvious answers are, "No" and "No."

I have never seen a person lying in a coffin looking anything close to natural or peaceful. Ever. It had to be said. And those observations have to stop being said out loud.

As far as my hair is concerned, I get anxious thinking about this for good reason. I have never, ever, ever left a hair salon with hair styled in a way I will ever, ever, ever wear again. I don't know what it is about getting my hair cut and styled, but I assume that when I walk in, the person can see how I have styled my hair.

Unless I say, "I hate this style, please change it," I assume they understand when I say, "Please just give me a trim; this style is working for me."

Apparently I now need to have them repeat back to me

what I have just said about my hair to them. To be safe, I also carry a photo of the haircut I want, which is a selfie taken minutes prior to the appointment.

I have left hair salons with bangs swooping across my forehead that make bad comb-overs look good. I have left hair salons with hair so stiffly back-combed, I gave Dolly Parton's wigs a run for their money. I don't like hair swooped on my face. Never have. Never will. Yet I have left hair salons with hair brushed so forward onto my face that I look like the cowardly lion from *The Wizard of Oz*.

I digress here, but I do worry greatly how my hair will be styled for my last appearance on this earth. I am now thinking if I do decide to be buried, I might suggest I wear the hood from my favorite sweatshirt on my head. Being buried seems to have lots of things to do to prep for viewing, and then into the ground I go.

Strange customs we have. Get all dressed up and really nowhere to go. I wonder if this is where that saying came from?

On to cremation. Kind of simple, really. No clothes, makeup, or hair plucking to worry about. No lying in a box on display, and no comments about how peaceful I look. Just take me, and off we go to the . . . to the . . .

Okay, so that's the part I can't say or think about. The "what happens to me after I die" part in cremation. I have to write something down about really making sure I am dead before you know . . . let's just leave it at: I would like three professional medical opinions, please.

I get it. Again, I won't be alive, so what difference does it make? But for some reason I get a little woozy thinking more about cremation, more so than being buried. And yet I don't want to be in a box down in the ground, either.

Other ideas? Anyone? Anyone?

Most people I know are planning to be cremated. My dad was. I was told his cremation went well, which is kind of unsettling to hear about someone you love. It's weird and proves the significance of the words we use around death. Being told the cremation went "well" can only mean that sometimes it doesn't.

There are so many variables to consider around dying and what happens to us after we die. Many emotions come to the surface when discussing death. For example, I know that when I get nervous, and talking about death stuff can make me slightly nervous, I laugh or find things inappropriately funny. I hear words differently or in a different context. This is illustrated by the time a gentleman from the mortuary was leaving with my dad's body. The man asked if my dad's apron was with him or on him.

Apron? Why would my dad need an apron on his way to being cremated? Why on earth would he be wearing an apron now?! Did he request that he be put in his apron upon death? I could only think of an apron worn in the kitchen, which I had never seen my dad wear. I found myself wondering was it a tie-around-the-waist kind? An over-the-neck apron with "Wine for the cook" written on it? Honestly, I was thrown off completely by the question to my dad's wife by the mortuary guy. I was also thrown off by his asking out loud and not in more of a hushed, someone-just-died tone. I was suddenly worried what his next question was going to be. I suddenly did not want to know what else my dad was wearing.

Turns out my dad was a Mason. There is a tradition of being cremated wearing a custom-adorned cloth tied around the waist, called, simply enough, an apron. This is a symbol for Masons and the custom is to wear the special apron with a sprig of evergreen tucked into the pocket part. The symbolism and custom elude me. I don't really know all of the details behind it. Honestly, it didn't matter.

I think more about dying now, and how my name is moving to the top of the list. It used to be that I could feel better knowing that a loved one who passed was so much older than me. I would find myself thinking, when someone died, in her seventies and above, that I still wasn't too close to that age. Well, now I am. Now some of my friends and family are, too. And further, some of my family and friends close to the age I am now have already made it to the other side. I have a creepy feeling that I need to be ready. I am not saying for what, just that I want to make sure I have done all the living I can absolutely pack into a life!

Simply being a woman of a certain age, I feel I am entering into territory that I need to know more about. Namely,

death. So I read the obituaries every week. I am mostly looking for people I know, but I am also reading about people's
lives. I like to read what they have done or liked to do. I am
also figuring out the average age of death based on the ages
given. Most weeks I am pretty close to that age, which scares
me a little.

I like having a sense of the person whose picture I see and
knowing how he or she passed. I also like to know that what
people did in their lives still matters. I mean, each person
has made a mark in this world, and now we are left with
what is written in their obituary? As I think more about this,
I realize obituaries are only snippets of a person's life. They
do not capture everything about a person. How could they?
Obituaries can make death and people's lives seem small
when nothing could be further from the truth. However, the
cost of obituaries might also explain a short life synopsis.

No matter which way I decide to handle my "after death"
arrangements, I understand I really won't be there. But if I
get a chance to watch from some celestial distance, I have
decided that I don't want to be zooming in on my hair. Or
my makeup. Or my outfit. Although if I do get to come back
and watch my funeral, that will be my inclination, I am sure.

Whether being buried or cremated, I am hoping that by
leaving this life and entering into what I believe is a much
higher plane of existence, I will become more elevated in
my thinking about what matters. I hope I will simply zoom
in on the flowers, the music, the words spoken, the magic

created by others gathering to celebrate my life, and all that it meant. I will most likely still have some leftover mortal desires and look at and judge the food being served after the service. Of course I will want to see my family again. Of course I probably should have put that first.

As far as I can tell there isn't one way to behave at a funeral. I used to think one dressed in all black and the tone was quite somber. People would speak in hushed tones and greet each other with hugs, kisses on the cheek, and a slight nod that said, "I know."

Only I never did know. I can talk in hushed tones, I have plenty of black stuff to wear as I find it somewhat slimming, and I can give people hugs for their loss. But what I can never figure out is the nod. Is it for "I know this is tough for you and loss is hard"? Or is it "I know, let's just get through this, and I will meet you back at the house for a few beers"?

As I have gotten older, I am more hopeful it is the second one.

I was ahead of the curve with preferring life celebrations to funerals. I am all for telling fun stories and laughing. Skip the somber tones and singing and bring on the dancing gypsies . . . or something like that. Please, I can't sit through any more sad eulogies and behave. Surely the person had their faults. Drank too much? Snored? Owed you money? We probably all knew this about them anyway, so I say tell the funny story. The one we can all relate to. More people would come to celebrate. It would be a very good time. Speaking of which, am I the only person who worries how many people will show up for their funeral? I have calculated numbers. I think a theme party will help to get more people to attend. Another thing to add to my healthcare directive?

I offer this idea of a life celebration versus funeral because, as I have mentioned, I am plagued with a problem of laughing at the most inappropriate of times. Someone dies, and it is too quiet at the funeral. I laugh out loud. If the unity candle won't light during a wedding service, I am the one laughing out loud and maybe saying, loud enough for a few to hear, "Uh-oh, it's a sign!" Someone in the choir sings off-key and I hear it . . . complete laughing breakdown. I am not proud of this.

Over the years my husband has forbidden me from leaning into him as I try to gain my composure from laughing too hard. He pushes me away; I laugh harder. He wants nothing to connect him to me. I understand. Often my children won't sit by me, either. Often I leave because I am going to wet my pants . . . yet another lovely reminder that I am of a certain age. This all brings me to, I want my party-themed funeral/life celebration to be a place where people can laugh freely and not be worried that it is inappropriate, and there will be several restrooms close by . . . in case. After all, if I were there, we now all know I would be laughing and crossing my legs!

Laughing aside, as I become more familiar with losing people and the experiences of that, I have realized quickly that there are not adequate words to completely describe what people go through during the death and dying process. This is true for the person dying as well as the person left behind. I also believe that to be able to experience the dying process with a loved one is a special, grace-filled gift. Losing someone quickly and without any indication is such a shock and can leave a different kind of heart imprint. A great reminder to say what you need to say while you can. Always.

Being with someone who is in the last part of his life brings forth questions. I mean, how do we say everything we want to and have it express the depth of the feelings we have? The feelings come from such a deep place within. Our given words are not enough. I find myself trying to find the right words, only I never think they are the right words. It is frustrating for me and I have fretted over capturing the perfect words to describe how much I have loved the person who was dying. I wanted to express how much I will miss the person and that life will feel so different. I began to wonder how I would ever know what to do, what to say. Then a friend once said to me, "Go to the source."

Of course, ask the person dying. That is what I would want.

Say What You Need to Say

"The reality is you will grieve forever. You will not 'get over' the loss of a loved one. You will learn to live with it. You will heal and you will rebuild yourself around the loss you have suffered. You will be whole again, but you will never be the same again. Nor should you be the same. Nor should you want to be." —Elizabeth Kübler Ross

I was with my dear brother-in-law, Tom, age sixty-four, as he lay in his hospice room bed, weighing hardly anything and barely fitting into his extra-small sweatshirt. It was close to his time of death. Either I or someone else would stay with him so he would not have to die alone. I knew he had that fear from a previous conversation we had. At the end, I was with him as much as I could be. Tom was like a close girlfriend, and I don't say that just because he was gay. He was a true best buddy in my life.

Simply put, Tom meant the world to me and I loved him dearly. We shared a friendship that allowed for frustration and love to be equally felt and expressed. He was one of the few people I could be totally honest with. He was in the circle of people I loved the most. And I was losing him.

While I spent those last, precious moments with him, I longed to say something meaningful that would give him comfort. But I could not think of anything to say that would fully represent the feelings I had for him. We had talked about death before. We were both believers in Heaven and all that is promised in our faith. But somehow being present in death made it harder to know what to say about it. I wanted to know how he was doing and what it felt like to be dying. We had talked about so many things along the way, so I had to ask myself why his dying should be any different.

I decided to take a risk and ask Tom what I wanted to know: "How you are feeling with death near? Are you scared? What is it like?"

He was silent for what felt like an eternity. I listened to the ticking of the clock that hung on the wall in his hospice room. Ironically I had never noticed it before that moment. The ticking seemed to be a heavy sound that filled the air, almost so much so that I couldn't breathe. It was as if time was becoming louder, reminding us to take advantage of what little time was left.

Tom finally answered my questions. And I finally took a breath.

"I am afraid," he said, as silent tears flowed gently down his face. He closed his eyes and turned away. With tears sliding softly down his gaunt, ashen face, he opened his eyes again and said, "Even though I know I'm dying, I don't want to say the words. I don't want to give any power to death just yet."

His breathing became lighter, and it seemed to give rhythm to the ticking clock. I thought he was asleep. I was left to my own thoughts.

I began to wonder how I could help him with his fear. I wanted to think about words I could say to lessen what he was feeling, but I could not think of one thing to say that would take away his fear. So I remained quiet and still.

Silence lasted for some time before my brother-in-law began talking again. "I believe I am going to a better place. That helps me when I start to think about what happens when I die. It's the knowing that I will never see you or anyone else I love on this earth again. That is what makes me sad. That is what makes me afraid."

I wasn't sure how this conversation should go or about the words needed to be said. I became aware of how my body was tensing; I wasn't able to move. I still couldn't come up with the right words. I wanted to be that person, the one who knew what to say and have great wisdom. But I didn't know what to say. So I told him I loved him and that I wished I had the perfect words to say for him at this moment.

He smiled, and I felt better.

I absolutely let go of trying to have any "right" anything, and we had one of the best conversations we ever had during his last days.

I asked him to tell me what it was like for him. "What are you thinking about? What does it feel like? And what questions do you have about dying?"

I took his lead by the way he would offer silence as he pondered the questions. I watched as he used his eyes to give me whatever emotion he could to express himself. I wanted to be fully present for someone I loved. I simply wanted him to know he was not alone.

I often find myself talking out loud to Tom as if he is still with me. I know he is gone, but I still want to process some things like our favorite reality shows and the outfit worn by so-and-so, and to recap snarky stories about certain people. As silly as it sounds, I have had wonderful conversations with him since he passed on. He has become my greatest listener. Truth be told, Tom was a great teacher to me. I never told him that. It is something I regret but have now taken as a lesson. Say what you need to say and say it often; don't wait, hoping you'll get it in before the last breath is taken. When the student is ready, the teacher will appear. Ironically, the dying process can be a great teacher. But I want to be clear: I am ready to learn . . . not die!

I will never be the same as I was before Tom died, but I can make myself better because of all that I received from him. I learned so much from him, from his living and his dying.

There is something freeing about not having all the answers or admitting we don't always know what to say. It takes us to a magical place of being able to wonder, question, and anticipate out loud with someone. Imagine what we could learn if we allowed ourselves to be fully present for every moment, including the moments in the dying process. The learning and teaching would never seem to stop. If we pay attention.

As it turns out, Tom was cremated. So no worries about outfits or hair.

He wanted his ashes "stirred in with the rest in the common crypt" (his words). And that is exactly what we did.

Two things to make note of regarding cremation: One, you receive the remains in a cardboard box. I find that weird. Something so sacred as the remains of a person, and it is given to you in a cardboard box. I don't know what I was thinking the remains would be coming in, but I never once thought it might be a cardboard box. Remains make a rattling noise when shaken as small bone bits bounce against the sides of the box. This was noticed while on a car ride around the city (which my husband did with his brother's ashes). I know. I thought that was weird, too. It was his way of spending time with him one last night.

Two, I really feel masks would be useful when pouring remains into a common crypt. I know it is supposed to be a sacred moment; however, I was taken aback by all the dust and powdery stuff swirling about. I had a hard time letting go that I had just inhaled a bit of my brother-in-law.

No matter how monumental moments are, there is always room for learning and laughing about something. Even death. It seems to be all about the perspective we bring to the occasion. However, if you bring the perspective "I should take everything seriously," fair warning, I will eventually laugh.

It's about Your Heart and Who It Beats For

Another one of my greatest lessons about death came from an unexpected place: a thrift store.

I had committed to volunteering at the local thrift store. I really didn't want to go. It was a Saturday after a long work-week; I wanted to sleep in, drink coffee on the deck outside, and not have to do anything. I find I am great at signing up for volunteering things when I have great energy and the event is about four or more months away. Everything sounds doable when it's four months away.

I decided to go. What would it say about me if I lied and said I was sick or something came up? Trust me. I considered this briefly. I mean, who would ever know besides me, right? I could blame not being able to help due to arthritis. No one ever questions that excuse. At least not out loud.

Meanwhile, I managed to pack up my bitterness and resentment, and I drove myself to the damn thrift store to volunteer.

Once at the counter, I found the work to be at a quick pace. That made it hard for me to talk to people, which turned out to be perfect for me, given my mood.

It was well into the afternoon when I met him. I cannot remember his name, so I will call him Jack.

Jack came into the store wearing shorts, white socks with stripes at the top, tennis shoes, a T-shirt with a logo on it, and a pair of glasses with a small chip in the lens on the left-hand bottom. All that aside, what really stood out was his personality and smile. He was probably in his sixties. He came in happily, announcing to me with a big ol' smile, "Hello! This is an adventure day for my girlfriend and me. We took the back roads to your thrift store. My girlfriend loves thrift stores, and I love taking back roads. Win-win for both of us."

He walked right up to the cash register. He put one hand down on the countertop, crossed his legs, and leaned on the counter. He smiled even bigger and began to tell me about how his day had started out. He spoke of how he was determined to make this a good day and not have any pre-set agenda. His smile and conversation were very contagious. I leaned in now, too.

We went on to talk about organized religion (seriously), the economy, his late wife and how much he loved her, his grandmother and her disdain for "those Catholics." He talked about how his girlfriend in high school (he loved her, too) had a dad that didn't like that he was Swedish, much less going out with his Norwegian daughter!

We talked about how he was going to use the vase he found at the thrift store to make a centerpiece for his table: "Put it on my girlfriend's (he loves this current girlfriend as much as he loved anyone; he told me over and over) tab when she comes up here." He smiled and winked.

Time seemed to stand still as he talked about his life.

There were no other customers in the store at the time Jack and his girlfriend stopped in. For the entire day, before and after they left, this never held true again.

I chuckled to myself thinking, *Geez, this guy is way over-sharing, and he sure has loved a few women along the way!* Yet, I also felt like he was sharing just the perfect amount. It was strange this dichotomy I was in. I felt very comfortable in a very personal conversation with someone I had never met before. In my mind, I proclaimed him to be a safe person to talk to. I noted he was an overall pretty upbeat guy. Not one to be wary of.

I told him I was appreciative of his conversation and how he was helping to make the time go by. His personality was so contagious. His smile made others smile. He had those great expressive eyes that drew me in. His wrinkles let me know he had shared many smiles over the years. I thanked him for stopping in, for adding to my day in such a great way, noting to myself that my mood had dramatically changed for the better.

Then he said, "I'm glad I helped make your day. That's all I want to do these days. I want to make great days for every-one, including myself because I am dying."

I was stunned.

Jack explained that he had a terminal type of cancer that Geraldine Ferrero died from. Peter Boyle had just died from it as well. I learned all about his cancer condition from him. He gave me more medical information, more than I could ever understand.

I noticed what I thought was a port in his chest when his T-shirt moved over a certain area on his chest. I assumed it was the entry point for his chemo. He noticed me looking there as well. I felt self-conscious for looking at it.

Jack looked down and touched his shirt covering his portal, then looked up and smiled at me. He leaned in again and said, "I want this day, and all the others I have left, to mean something and to be an adventure. I am lucky. I know that I am dying. I know my time is limited. I'm living with that knowledge and to not make the most of the time I have left would be a shame."

He paused for a minute and said, "The thing is, everyone knows they are going to die. But not many of us live life the way we should. We take time and others for granted. Life is so precious. So remember, life is what you make it."

What do I say to that? What could I offer? I felt so humbled by his simple, yet powerful words. His girlfriend came up with her purchases. He asked her if he talks too much.

She laughed and said, "You should always bring your duct tape with you!"

He put his arm around her, she leaned into him, and they began to walk away. He turned to me before he left.

I quickly said something I have never said to a stranger before, "I will lift you up. I will pray for you."

He smiled that great smile of his and said, "Yes, pray for me. Please pray for me, and I will pray for you as well." I saw the sunlight in his tears that fell down his cheek. He waved, paused, and then told me to make the most of my days.

The tears came to my eyes, too. I was overcome by a power so much greater than me. Just then I realized I had been in the presence of Grace. I had been wrapped by a power and force so great. It didn't matter that I had never met him before. I knew him now. By Jack choosing to stop in the thrift shop that day, my life changed. I received a great blessing that started out with something as small as saying, "Hello."

He left the store, but his imprint made a permanent mark on me and perhaps others as I remember what he said about living my life in the best way I can. After him, I greeted every person differently that came into the thrift shop. My day was filled with wonderful people and their stories. I learned and felt so much more than I would have had I not met Jack. I just know it.

We will never know what could happen to shorten our lives. Death is unavoidable. However, we will never know who we might meet in a day or how we might be blessed, just by saying a simple hello. We need to ask ourselves, not knowing where our names are on the waitlist, are we living the width as well as the length of our life? Our answer is very important.

I have no idea what happened to Jack after he left the thrift shop. I assume he passed on shortly thereafter. But I also assume he enjoyed a well-lived life all the way to the end. What I do know is that it is a privilege to be touched by others in a way that helps us to see the beauty, the magic all around us. We will never be too old to experience that. We will never be so close to dying that we can't experience a connection with others. I am grateful for being able to volunteer at the thrift store that particular day. And I will always be grateful for meeting Jack.

Sometimes You Say Good-bye Before They Are Gone

"I felt like I was pulling a movie screen down and watching a film of myself every time I was with my brother as he became even more lost in his Alzheimer's. It was scary. It still is scary for me. I worry all the time I will have Alzheimer's."

These words came from a woman named Jane, age sixty-five, when discussing the loss of loved ones with Alzheimer's and fears about her own mortality.

The idea of experiencing someone with memory loss or worries about their own memory loss was high on the list of topics I had with many women I interviewed. It seemed that if a woman had experiences with someone close having Alzheimer's or another form of a diagnosable memory loss condition or dementia, the fear of "getting it" themselves was quite high.

Jane summed this up by saying, "It used to be common to forget something every now and then. Now when I forget something I worry it's the beginning of Alzheimer's. I worry since my brother had it, I will, too."

Carolyn, age fifty-eight, said, "When I forget someone's name I think, *Oh my God, it's happening to me.*" She said that her mother has Alzheimer's and it has been a tough road. She added, "Now when I am around my mom I wonder whenever I can't remember something if I am starting to show signs of early onset. Rationally I know I'm not, but emotionally I worry. I had to ask my husband and kids to stop telling me, 'I already told you that.'"

It seems that no matter how well we take care of ourselves, there are still issues that lurk inside our bodies that do not make themselves known until we are older. Alzheimer's and other forms of dementia continue to scare many of us, especially as we age. The truth is, it is damn scary because it feels like there is nothing we can do about it.

Many women shared their experiences taking care of a loved one with Alzheimer's.

Gail, age sixty-five, said, "My mom knew me up until a month before she passed. I had to emotionally detach from her in order to continue to care for her. I said good-bye to her long before she passed. She was not my mom anymore."

Jane added, "I also had to remember my brother was long gone before he died. His passing was a relief, but also it was so sad for me. It's almost like they leave you twice. It was brutal to leave my brother in the nursing home. He would pound on the window sobbing, watching me get in my car in the parking lot. He seemed to remember me then, even for a small moment of time. It was so hard."

She added, "I had a friend tell me she prayed for her sister who had Alzheimer's to die. I completely understood and felt nothing but compassion for her."

Violet, age sixty-seven, talked about her mother and discovering her mom had the early stages of Alzheimer's. "It started out as me getting irritated each time my mom forgot something and I had to repeat myself several times in one conversation. I thought she was just talking out loud and making triple sure she got the details right; she can be overly detailed. I continued to be irritated with her calling me back several times after talking about something only to re-ask me questions about what we had just talked about. I felt so frustrated with her. Now I know it was the beginning of her Alzheimer's, and I still feel awful I didn't know what was really going on."

Violet became quiet for a moment, seeming to gather herself, and then she shared more. "I see myself as kind and patient with others. What I am so ashamed about is how I could not find that for my own mom. I mean, it got to the point where I would not answer her phone calls or, if I did, I would say my cellphone was losing battery charge and I had to hang up. I felt that I didn't have it in me to keep repeating myself and trying to help her remember the simplest things. I would hang up and yell, swear, and cry. I knew something was not right, but it took almost two years before I began to put it all together. I did some research. That was when I realized her symptoms were typical with Alzheimer's. One of my biggest regrets is that I moved away, figuratively, from her, not toward her. Who does that?"

She said her mom continues to struggle with her memory and at present they have not been able to convince her that she needs help. At least they are talking about it as a family. Violet seems resolved to continue to push for a medical evaluation, but realizes that for some Alzheimer's patients it takes a crisis before more help and action can be taken. Obviously that is something Violet does not want to happen. And yet she might not have a choice.

What an incredible dilemma to be in. I believe her when she said she will continue to try and help her mom as best she can and that it is some of the hardest work she will ever do. I think everyone at this particular women's gathering wanted to help both Violet and her mom. Our hearts broke. My heart broke for all the women who shared their stories of losing a loved one not once, but twice, to Alzheimer's.

As I listened to women speak of their experiences dealing with Alzheimer's or other forms of dementia, I was so struck by the guilt felt by many of them. Many stories included not wanting to be with their loved one once the disease completely overtook them and the guilt they felt because of that.

One woman named Roxanne, age seventy-one, talked of how her husband became combative and would swear at her during his end of life with Alzheimer's. She wondered out loud how someone could become so different than what they were in their life before Alzheimer's. She said, "My husband was not the same man I married. But how could I not love him? I loved my husband dearly before he got sick. I felt more sorry for my husband than love after he got sick."

She added in a whisper with tears quietly running down her cheeks, "How does Alzheimer's happen anyways?"[3]

No one in the room had anything to say. No one knew what to say. Gentle tears of compassion fell from the others in the room. A couple of women offered a hand and hug for comfort. Watching and listening to Roxanne and having experienced a few others sharing their stories along the way, I believed not having any words was exactly what was needed.

Driving Mr. Daisy

The year before I turned fifty began with my dad passing away. It wasn't enough to begin losing my youth; now I was placed in the position of losing a parent. It was another symbolic way to seal the deal. I was, indeed, getting older. My name was inching up on the list as other names were removed.

My dad was diagnosed with lung cancer caused by mesothelioma. Essentially he died from asbestos eating away at

3 To make a donation or to find out more information about Alzheimer's, contact www.alz.org.

his lungs. He was also a smoker.

The fact that he smoked and had lung cancer incensed me to no end. He tried to quit. Looking back, I know it was very hard for him. It was his addiction, and he had a hard time giving up nicotine. And really, who could blame him? He knew he was dying after his diagnosis, so why quit then?

I remember thinking that if he quit I would at least feel like he was fighting back and not giving the cancer any extra help in killing him. But with anyone we love, finding blame as to why they are leaving us seems to help. It seems to give us a place to put the anger we have.

I went with my dad to his oncology appointments. I shared driving times with my sister, and sometimes we all went together. I would never trade this time spent with my dad and my sister for anything. It may sound strange, but I found being with my dad in the car, and knowing he was in the dying process, forged a strong sense of kinship between us. I actually found myself looking forward to picking him up and driving him to the doctor's office. Even if I knew our only outing was to the oncologist's office.

There is something about car rides that can bring out the best in people. It was always the one time my kids would really open up to me. I found out about friendships, worries, and joys. It must be the captive time and maybe the fact that we don't have to look at each other face to face. I am not completely sure. But the same magic happened with my dad and me in our car rides.

During one ride, my dad said very unexpectedly, "To be your dad is one of the proudest things I have accomplished in my life. You, along with your sister, are my greatest gifts to this world. Make sure you don't wait as long as I have to tell your own children this."

I won't forget. I haven't.

We drove the rest of the way in silence. There were no more words to say. It was one of his last gifts to me before he passed on.

As my dad moved into hospice care, I knew the end would be near. Our time pretending that he was doing okay was over. My dad had held onto taking care of himself probably for too long. He was a proud and stubborn man.

My dad died on a beautiful fall day. The sun was shining, and sunlight danced off the colors from the fall leaves scattered about, creating a kaleidoscope effect all around. This created a magical effervescence all around the room where my dad took his last breath. I was there when he took it. There was an indescribable feeling that came over me as I knew he was walking to the other side.

Being with someone as they pass over is a sacred time. I felt I'd walked a little bit along with my dad and my dear friend Tom as they left. I can only describe it as the room feeling different, and the air was heavier. I knew then and I know now, I was in a place of Grace. I was in a place filled with such sacredness as my dad passed that even now I am still at a loss for words. The feeling defies description.

When I leave this worldly place, I hope my children will be able to feel the Grace I experienced when my dad died. It helps me to feel somewhat settled in what can be an unsettling situation.

So What Did I Learn?

After all of this, I still do not know if I will be buried or cremated. I am not sure I should even be the one to decide on this anymore. I have also decided not to ask friends what they are doing anymore. It all causes me too much stress. I would hate thinking about what to do with me after I die had anything to do with me dying! I have read the studies about stress and links to death. To feel better prepared, I will leave notes about considerations for me after I die. Whatever is decided, I do want to have it done with me wearing my favorite sweatpants outfit. No matter how I end up, buried or cremated, I want to be comfortable. No exceptions. This idea gives me some peace.

Here is what I do know. As I think of my death, I have been given some clarity around what is important while living. It is all about the relationships we have. Whether for a small period of time or a lifetime, how we treat others, even those we may only meet once, is how we leave our imprint in this world. No one will remember that great pair of shoes we had and wore only twice because they hurt too much. Or the hairstyles we had and paid too much for. What others remember about someone is the way we made them feel. We can't cover that up with a cute outfit and shoes. So as I get older and become even more a "woman of a certain age," I will resign to live in a way so that when others remember me when I am gone they will say, "She always made me feel comfortable and loved."

And in keeping with my dad's request, I say to my children: "To be your mom is one of the proudest things I have accomplished in my life. You are my greatest gifts to this world."

It turns out I share one of my brother-in-law's worries: I am not afraid of losing things, places, people, or even death itself. When it comes right down to it, I will simply feel sad to say good-bye.

In gratitude for being able to love someone
so much it makes saying good-bye
that much harder to do.
(Thank you, Winnie the Pooh!)

CHAPTER 6

I Got This, Right?

"The longest journey still begins with one step." Or as my kids would say: "It's not THE *Google, it's just Google!"*

I HAVE THINGS I simply enjoy doing, and others I do not.

I believe this comes from my desire to only do things I am comfortable with. Over time, lots of time has fluttered past me, and I find I settle into a pattern of doing those things I truly believe I am either good at or comfortable with.

I am not one to challenge myself for many new adventures. That isn't to say I believe people of a certain age should shut down all new opportunities or new adventures. In fact, I have met a few people of a certain age that have just begun to try out their exploratory wings. One acquaintance of mine began making lovely pieces of pottery after she turned sixty. Her pottery is being exhibited in a variety of art shows. Her dream of being an artist has finally come true, and she could not be happier!

Another person I know became certified as a yoga instructor at the fine age of fifty-seven. She was tired of attending a class where she was one of the oldest participants. She now runs yoga classes for women fifty and older, her business is booming, and participants can practice the lotus in comfort and without judgment.

Another person I know is getting back into the work force at age eighty-four. She wants to stay productive and continue to contribute to society. She decided to get a job in a greeting card store. She told the person interviewing her that she was bored and wanted to get out and about more. That and she knew how to make a great sale. Indeed. She was a former sales representative for a major corporation and had managed to get the company in the Fortune 500 Club. She figured if she could negotiate a major international sales contract, she could certainly sell greeting cards! She reports being thrilled by having a job that allows her to wear outfits that had been hanging in her closet for too long. I love her.

These and many, many more examples of women of a certain age participating in exciting, new adventures allow me to feel safe in believing that it is never too late to do and become what I really want to become.

Many women believe that as we age we need to settle and not take as many risks. We succumb to the myth that once we reach a certain age, it's all over but the shouting! Not true. A woman name Jocelyn, age fifty-nine, shared, "I was laid off last year. Not having a job and for me, a work-related purpose, was harder than I thought it would be. It took a lot out of me. I missed my work environment and feeling like I was contributing. I was very good at my job, and it brought me satisfaction. I have a new job now but it has been hard to learn everything new. It has me wondering if employers really want to ever hire older people." She offered a pause and said, "I really am looking forward to retirement. I just want it to be when I am ready."

Another woman at the same gathering said, "As I listened to what you said I realized that I feel invisible sometimes. I can be in a restaurant and it seems like the entire wait staff go to the younger, more fun tables to get their orders. My husband and I end up waiting much longer than it seems we should. We have even commented on feeling like we are not just the boomer generation, but now the invisible generation."

These comments and many others like them have me reflecting on how Western society may have lost out by not giving more value to aging and harvesting the wisdom learned from those of us over fifty. Based on all of the beautiful, smart, and fun women I have been meeting aged fifty and older, it is a shame to not tap into this rich and available resource.

While aging can bring a wealth of knowledge and experience, it can also give us a chance to see things from a "looking back" perspective as well as a "I am willing to learn more" perspective. Our experiences have bought us some freedoms in making decisions. We no longer have to ask those who have gone before; we are those people!

Age brings beautiful, delightful wisdom. Wisdom that creates a sense of "We got this, and this, and this and this." As a woman of a certain age named Linda said, "I feel smarter and wiser now. I am happier now. My life is actually pretty great now!"

I would say Linda has "got this!"

Sometimes when we do not take any more risks or try new things as we age, we may succumb to complacency. One example is having a sedentary lifestyle. Our day can become guided by the shows that are on TV or the times of our meals. Routine becomes a pattern, and the pattern can destroy our life. This is when being invisible is felt the strongest. Of course, I am not talking about having medical conditions here. Those often require some sort of routine to manage symptoms or conditions. And as we age that is certainly something to take into consideration.

However, I am writing about the way in which we stay locked into a pattern of living or thinking. The kind of living that doesn't allow for variations. I have no medical journal to quote here, but I know my wisdom gleaned over the years in watching women who age is—if they don't move it, they lose it. Mind, body, and spirit.

All of it needs to move and be moved.

To get started, we must challenge our mind-set. What

have we allowed ourselves to become? And, more importantly, where do we want to go, and what do we need to change to make that happen? What work do we need to do that we might be afraid to do, to make the changes necessary to live the life we want to lead?

Simply put, "The first step of change is to become aware of your own bullshit."—Spirit Science.

So . . . we start sorting through the mess and take the risk. Make the necessary changes to live the life we really want today. The longest journey really does start with the first step.

When You Stand on a Platform, You See More

My new challenge at this age is being a writer. I always secretly knew I wanted to write. I never believed I could or should. And then it hit me. If I don't start now, then when will I? Time is certainly ticking a little more loudly these days. So I jumped into the writing world. Both feet. By becoming a writer I also became a pseudo technology wizard. I had no idea how to navigate technology, but I became a quick (well, really not that quick) learner.

Side note: if you ever want to feel old, start by asking someone younger about how to operate technology. It makes us painfully aware of how we might have talked to our younger children. The tone is too schmaltzy, slightly condescending, and there is an overuse of the question, "Does this make sense?"

I don't know what it is, but my brain does not seem to be wired for working technology. It is as if there is a silent cut-off for people over a certain age on how to successfully engage in using technology.

Having said that, however, technology challenges continue to be on my list of new things to try. While not one of my strong suits, IT is more about trying to keep up. Every time I master a new technological device or application, it seems something new takes its place, or it becomes obsolete (or at least that is what my kids tell me). I always thought AOL dialup was here to stay. And oh, how I loved my Walkman.

Moving along, I have joined the techno world in several ways. I currently have a website, a Facebook page, and a LinkedIn page, and I use Twitter. Using social media takes quite a bit of time and energy to keep updated. Not to mention trying to develop a platform as a writer, which I found out is very important. I never knew to use this word in the technology or writing world until I decided to write a book.

I simply wanted to write a few thoughts about getting older, offer some insight into the need for changing how we view aging in our culture, and tell a few funny, hopefully relatable stories. Turns out you need a platform. I had to ask: what is this so-called platform, and why would I need one?

I attended a writer's conference in San Francisco and one of the few questions I was asked, no matter whom I spoke with, was, "How is your platform?"

I made stuff up. I had no idea what they were talking about. It wasn't until a breakout session that the question was finally asked, not by me, but by another woman of a certain age: "What is this platform that everyone is talking about? What did I miss?"

Oh, there was such a sigh of relief in the room, or maybe it was just me who exhaled a little too loudly. No matter, I finally learned what platform meant, and what that meant for me as a writer. And it was then I knew I had to learn even more about technology. There is a saying, "It's hard to teach old dogs new tricks," for a reason. And I was determined not to be that old dog.

In case you are wondering, a platform is all about building the numbers of people interested in what you are doing, working on, or have to say. This can include Facebook, Twitter, and other social media. I would also add as an introvert I would rather have pink eye than ask people to "follow me."

I decided to try a class that would help me build my platform. To make it even more challenging, I decided to take the class online. I was excited. And nervous. And not sure it was a good idea by the day the class was to begin. It was more like: *What was I thinking? I am not technologically savvy in the least!*

Then I remembered a favored saying, "You don't have to see the whole staircase to climb it; just take the first step."

Thank you, Dr. Martin Luther King, Jr.

My first task was to set up access to the program, allowing me to be visible and communicate to the other students taking this class. I started working on this three days prior. Since the program could not be activated until the actual class, I never really knew if it was working or would work. I received an email and a pop-up saying I was activated. And to be safe, I had two of my three children, a colleague at work, and someone I knew who worked in the technology world look at it. They said I was ready.

I wrote down all of the instructions and steps to do in order to be active the night of the class. I should have been ready to go. So I waited. Waited. And waited a bit more for class to begin.

After all that waiting and prepping, prepping and waiting, I missed the first class. Was I sick? No. Did something come up preventing me from attending the online class? No. Was it a technology glitch after all? No. It was simply a matter of me not recognizing the time difference between Pacific and Central time zones. All of the prepping, practicing, and anxiety over taking my first online class, and I missed it!

What made me realize this, you ask? I sat in front of my computer after brushing my teeth and hair, cleaning up any mess that could be seen in the background from the camera in my computer, and setting up my desk to look like I was organized, yet casual. Nothing came on screen. By all accounts I was set up for the online class. I checked and rechecked several times. I sat there five, fifteen, and then twenty minutes before I emailed the teacher. This after I yelled into the screen wondering if anyone could hear me, just maybe not see me and vice versa. Four times I did this. I had an idea:

Subject Line: *HELP!* (From Kim Kane, student)

Hello So and So.

I am trying desperately to attend your online class this evening. Unfortunately my computer screen is blank. Can you help me by giving me suggestions to get on for the next class? If possible, and if there is a lull in your teaching yet this evening, could you respond to me with any suggestions so I might be able to still attend a portion of your class this evening?

Thank you in advance for your help. I am so looking forward to attending your class.

Kim

While waiting for a response, I continued to futz with the computer. I emailed the company who provided the service to receive the online class. They assured me that I had an open account, and everything should be working on their end. Perhaps the teacher had problems with her connection, they suggested.

Oh, I never thought of that! Maybe it wasn't me after all. What a relief that it could be a problem with someone else or . . . I was exhausted from thinking of all the possibilities. I went to bed. After all it was 8:30 and I had been lamenting for over an hour and a half about this.

Early the next morning, I read the teacher's response email:

Hello Kim!

I am so sorry you missed our class last evening. I believe the reason is due to a misunderstanding of the time. I am in the Pacific Time zone, and when I said 5:00 p.m. for the class to begin, that is 7:00 p.m. for you. You might have missed the information on time zone difference in the last couple of emails I sent out as a reminder. As I teach this class for people all across the country, I base the time on the zone I am in.

I hope this helps. I look forward to you joining us next week for class.

As a reminder it will begin at 7:00 p.m. YOUR TIME.

Let me know if there is anything else I can help with.

Best regards,

So and So

My head became filled with those self-sabotaging thoughts of: I am never going to get this. There is too much to take in. I am pretty sure my head is already filled up with too much information to be able to take in any more. Especially technology. I wondered if, along with some clothing items, I might actually be allergic to technology as well?

I went on like this for a while. I reminded myself I had paid for this class and because I paid with a credit card, I could not write a grocery store name in the check register for my husband to see. Somehow he would figure out I paid for a class I never took. I better suck it up and figure this out. I began to take stock of what I knew.

Good news: I was really ready to go for this class. Technology and all. Job well done!

Bad news: I am having trouble remembering some things. Like time zone differences.

Good news: I will no longer take classes online with different time zones.

Bad news: After reading the response email, my entire body became flushed from embarrassment. This started the mother of all hot flashes and lasted well into the night.

Good news: I was never late to another class after that.

For those of us not used to all the technology stuff, we tend to shy away from it. We might even declare it something that is ruining lives. What I know for sure is that it is here to stay. So either hop on board, or sit back and watch the world go by. Luckily, I don't think it is all or nothing. I really do want to get into the game, but I also do not want technology to run my life. So I try a few new things. Like many of us, I stick my feet into the water and see if it is okay. If not, I quickly draw them back in and move on. If all is well, I stay and continue to move farther into the proverbial water.

Once I got the time right for my online class, it was full steam ahead. One of a few things I took note of from my first class (really the second class) was that the dim lighting in my office made it slightly hard for the other participants to see me online. Even though I prefer mood lighting to lessen the probability of showcasing facial flaws, I ended up changing the bulb wattage. I added a lovely rose-tinted bulb that seemed to enhance versus show too much. I also noticed I needed to keep the computer up slightly higher than normal so my second, and sometimes third, chin was not in the camera shot. I thought about wearing a scarf. No matter; these were easy fixes. No one else needed to know. However, this begs the question: does anyone else have these thoughts? I mean, am I the only one who worries about lighting, double chins, and whether my background looks tidy? Have I always worried about this, or is it simply another reminder of my aging?

Again, those are the easier fixes that no one else but me is aware of. Then there are the fixes that everyone will know about. My friend, my foe . . . technology!

One of the tasks of the class was to write out our marketing statement, our desired goals, and what would be our tag line. This was to be posted on a group Facebook page for all to see and give feedback to. The instruction I missed was the timing piece. Again with the time issue.

Living by that motto of being prepared now, I smugly entered my information on the page before class. I was so proud to have completed the task and to understand how to utilize the technology tools. I even knew how to upload my logo onto the page. Big, big gains for me! Honestly, I was so delighted with my accomplishment.

But that was short-lived.

Once class began, I was immediately notified via IM (instant messaging) from the teacher to please remove my information from the Facebook page. It wasn't my turn. "Would you mind just waiting until your turn and then place all of the information on then? Someone else was scheduled to go first."

My first instinct was again to simply hit "delete" and get out of the class. I really wanted out immediately. I saw on the Facebook page the question posed from the person who was supposed to go first, wondering out loud to everyone in the class if they should wait and let me go first.

"No!" I typed back. "I will fix this. I am removing it now. So sorry!"

I panicked. I highlighted all of my work and hit "delete." I realized at the very moment I hit "delete" that I never saved any of that work. Not any of it.

I sat back, took myself off camera, and allowed myself to feel the embarrassment, flushing and all. It would be okay. I would be okay. It took me a minute, but along with feeling the embarrassment, I allowed myself to keep perspective. I am a student who is learning. I do not need to have all the answers, experiences, or knowledge of all things. It really would be okay. And it had nothing to do with my age. I was simply learning about something new. I got this.

I sent an IM to the teacher explaining to her what had happened, and secondly, asking her if she was going to kick me out of the class. She assured me I was welcome to stay and that she wanted me to stay. She also went on to teach me how to recover my information. In fact, she went to the online class to take a minute to explain it to all of us in case this happens to anyone in the future . . . and she used the words, "Because it will happen in the future to all of us."

I felt a solid sense of belonging. This prompted a host of very insightful pieces of information to be shared by all of my classmates. I was even contributing to the conversation in a smart way. It was awesome and so helpful. All of us commented on how nice it was to know others had struggles in various areas in the technology world.

Most importantly, I was not alone, and I was not the technology loser I had thought a few times. This old dog was learning some new tricks after all. It is never too late for any of us . . . ever. After class that night, I couldn't help but think, *Yeah, I got this.*

However, for many of us as we age there is a worry that we no longer "got this," whether it is due to the work force changes with younger women coming in, the ads in magazines highlighting younger women as their target audience, or even the way in which others address us (Ma'am). Our belief that others are treating us differently now that we are (getting) older is created. It becomes a mind-set for many of us.

The point is, we cannot glean who we are or what we are capable of by other's beliefs or standards. We need to create our sense, our own belief, and live those.

Yeah, we're aging, and yeah, we still got this!

"As you get older you will understand more and more that it is not about what you look like or what you own. It's all about the person you've become." —Christiane Northrup, MD.

Well, Ms. Northrup, in keeping with your words, I do believe I am becoming something of a technology wizard!

In Case You Need a Mantra, Repeat After Me: Wrong Tour Group

I love older homes and was pleased to have received a Mother's Day gift from my oldest son to go on a walking tour of older homes in an upscale old neighborhood. What a treat for me not only to see the houses but also to spend some time with my son.

The day of the walking tour was quite cold. I decided to wear my down jacket, mittens, and a scarf. I packed my boots in the car in case I decided it was too cold to walk about in just my tennis shoes. When I arrived, I picked up the tickets at the will call desk and proceeded to text my son that I had the tickets, and I would meet him inside when he got there. He replied that he was running late and would be there shortly.

"No problem," I texted. I then shut off my ringer.

I heard the receptionist announce to the group that the tour would begin in the drawing room and to take a seat and wait for the tour guide. Perfect.

The tour guide was dressed in a period piece. She was obviously very delighted to be our guide and very knowledgeable about this particular house. I began to wonder if we would have a different tour guide in each home, or if she would be the one to take us to each new house. I also wondered if she would be wearing a coat. I looked around and saw another woman clearly needing help walking and only dressed with a sweater over her blouse. This walking tour might be too much for her. I knew I was judging her and her clothing choice, but I couldn't help think she would get cold without a coat. Even though I was getting sweaty, I knew that when we went outside I would be dressed appropriately. Of course I also wondered if I should share my scarf with her. But I really didn't want to.

After a wonderful monologue about the history of the family who lived in this particular house and how the room we were sitting in was used back in the day, we were asked to move into the next room. By now I was a little more worried for my son missing out on the tour, and less about the woman not having a coat to wear. I was also having some questions pop up about what this tour was actually about.

Were we going to first tour this house and then go to the others? Were we only going to see the first floor of this house and then leave? Why was I the only person in a down jacket, gloves, and a scarf?

Things weren't adding up. I started to get that feeling where I feel I am not where I am supposed to be or doing what I am supposed to be doing. It's that place in my brain that opens up like a fog machine and everything seems blurry. I am cognizant of my surroundings, but much like when I forget where I parked the car, I cannot comprehend all information. A slight panic set in.

I started to run through the Rolodex of information in my mind.

Right date and time? Check. Correct place? Check. Tickets with correct names on them? Check. Woman at front desk announces for us to meet in drawing room. Check. What am I missing? And where the heck is my son?!

As we continued on to the next room, I decided to text my son again. I look down and see that I had several texts from him already.

"Mom, where are you?"

"Mom???"

"I'm here outside with the tour group. Where are you?"

I text back, "I am right here. I am in the house still."

Then it dawns on me like a blazing firework: *I AM in the wrong tour group?*

By then my fog machine starts to subside, and I at least

know where I am not supposed to be. By the time I put it all together, so has my son. I start to head toward the door, and he is already there.

"Wrong tour group," we say in unison.

We ran (I mostly trotted), laughing the whole way, to the right tour group about a half a block away. I forgot to put on my boots. Good thing. Boots and running do not mix. To be honest, running and I do not mix, with or without boots.

Being in the wrong tour group (WTG) serves as a great metaphor of how I feel as I age. I often feel misplaced in a world where things move fast or conversations happen that I know nothing or remember nothing about. I look around to see a familiar glance of someone else that might be feeling the same. And because I look around more, I see more. I am not sure if I feel better or worse, but I do feel included. I feel like I am in the right tour group.

There are glimpses of hope and joy to take from being in the WTG.

One is: always find time to be with family. I am my best self with my family. There is laughter, joy, and warmth that fill my soul when I am with those I love the most. Make the time to spend time with those you love. Appreciate them. Give thanks for them. Let all that happens be a part of the future memory of the experience. Make fun and create the fun of things unexpected. If you are doing something that causes some embarrassment, highlight it. If we keep things a secret or change the experience in a way that takes away the behavior or event because we think it shows a flaw in us, then that is on us. It's okay. By telling our story, we are giving value to others who have had similar situations. We create the norm around what we experience as we age.

Another nugget of the WTG is: enjoy the moment. Even though I was in the wrong tour group, I loved every minute of it. I enjoyed the tour guide, the history given, and the beauty of the house I was touring. Even though I became distracted at times by the questions rolling around in my head, I was moved by the stories shared about the family who had lived in the house and their celebrations held in the very room we visited. I allowed myself to be swept up in the magic of it all.

We must practice staying in the moment. That is all we have. I tend to be a "What if?" thinker. I am practicing becoming a "What now?" thinker.

Something very important to be taken from this WTG story is the power of humor. Laughing at ourselves is one of the best things we can do in many situations. Over all of the interviews I did, humor found its way into the conversation every time. Women spoke of the power of laughing even in situations where laughing would not always be seen as appropriate. Finding something funny took away the soul-blocking negativity. Finding the funny helps to reduce the stress caused by thinking everything went wrong or that we are not able to do something the "right" way.

My best stories come out of not doing things right. It has

led to some of the best laughter fits shared with family and friends. Bringing humor to the situation always helps. If you have done something embarrassing along the way, share it. You might be surprised at how many others have also been in the wrong tour group.

There is something so cathartic about being able to be vulnerable and sharing something we did that was funny. Being in the wrong tour group only makes us human. It shows we are vulnerable, not incapable. It makes us approachable. I want to remember this most of all as I age. It's okay to laugh at myself. There will be changes on the horizon that will be uncomfortable, but I am confident that keeping humor will help me keep perspective.

As Jennifer so perfectly stated, "I might lose my eyesight, hearing, and ability to always make it to the bathroom . . . but I do not want to lose my sense of humor."

Amen to that.

Because I have shared this story with many, I use the words "wrong tour group" for other experiences where I made a mistake. And I use this to showcase what exciting, beneficial things can happen by being in the wrong tour group.

I used to walk into a room full of people and wonder if they liked me. Now I look around and wonder if I will like them.

Before being in the wrong tour group, I worried about being invisible, having less value, and my voice seeming smaller. If I didn't have something profound to say, like Maya Angelou would, who would seek my wisdom? I succumbed to thinking that getting older meant becoming weaker in mind, body, and spirit. Now I know that being in the WTG is sometimes the best thing that can happen to me. It helps me to grow even stronger.

There is the saying, "Birds of a feather flock together," but there is also something to be said about being in the wrong flock. It can be wonder-ful and wonder-filled!

Tick, Tock, Well . . . Look at the Clock!

Thinking about what will change in our bodies, finances, or careers in the future was not something to spend time on. Until it was.

I remember being asked to be a contract negotiator for my work group. I was young and knee deep in having children and all that comes with that. My thought was to look into more pay and make sure we had sufficient health coverage. However, halfway into the negotiating process I was asked by colleagues I represented, "What are we going to negotiate with regard to retirement packages?"

Huh? It had never occurred to me to ask about retirement. In fact, many of their questions confused me. What would our premiums be after retirement? What benefit package would be offered to those with so many years under their belt? Would there be different packages to go with the different number of years a person had worked? And long-term care. What would the management offer in that package? Long-term care? *Why even bring that up?* I wondered.

Turns out these are very good questions to be asking in a work contract negotiation. But I sure didn't think so in those early years as a negotiator.

In the blink of an eye, my priorities changed when I became closer to retirement age. I, too, started to ask some of these questions. The younger group I represented was much more interested in pre-tax childcare dollars, pay, and vacation time. The rest of us wanted to know more about healthcare, our retirement accounts, and what the management would agree to contribute in that fund. Those two ends of the spectrum were often in competition for the dollars available. When I was younger I thought those older employees were retiring soon, and so shouldn't we be focusing on those who are staying? Now I think the younger staff will be there for longer; shouldn't we be focusing on those leaving soon? It's all about perspective and, as it turns out, planning. Or not planning.

Finances and retirement funds found their way into many conversations in the women's gatherings. One woman struck me in particular who shared her concerns around being able to retire. Karen is in her sixties and still working as a hairdresser. She spoke of not having any pension, and she is no longer married. At present her greatest hope is that she might be able to live with her son and his family.

"Maybe living with them means in a tiny house in their driveway!" she joked.

We all sensed her worry. I wondered how many others share her worry and even her joke. Karen works with many older ladies and enjoys the work she does, but her knees and back ache a little more and she isn't finding the needed stamina she used to have. Yet she still remains hopeful that everything will turn out for her. She stated, "I believe if I give, I will get back. It's that simple. I have always been taken care of and expect that I always will."

Her words gave great pause for many of us.

Barbara Lee added, "I don't worry about money, either. A couple of years ago my therapist said maybe I should. The truth is, if I did think about it I would be worried. I don't want to worry."

After being on the contract negotiation team years ago and remembering the conversations about planning for retirement, I find myself reading articles in the AARP magazine about how to save money even now. What I could afford to save in the past were not promising amounts, but I understood the merit to the saying, "A penny saved is a penny earned."

I no longer need to wonder about childcare dollars or even vacation time. I am busy figuring out what I can expect for my retirement dollars. Looking into ways to save money, I soon discovered it means staying away from items I consider sort of frivolous, but possibly necessary (lattes, several shades of lipsticks, and extra pairs of reading glasses).

And I find myself wishing I were younger. Again. No judging, please.

When I was younger and did not worry about money running out, I used to wear shoes with heels. I loved the look of how an outfit would be accessorized with a pair of good pumps. I felt taller and more stylish. Those of us who wore heels know the difference between a good, comfy pair of heels and ones that are not. Non-comfy heels were only to be worn in a short, make-a-statement time frame. Now I wear sensible shoes, ones that are not considered frivolous. I'm not saying they're not stylish; I am saying comfort is more important. These are shoes made just for stretching at the right places for bunions or swollen feet at the end of the day. Shoes with peep holes that allow air to circulate more readily, and shoes with rubberized soles to help minimize the potential for slipping while walking. All very necessary for me as I age. Nothing frivolous here.

You should have seen my shoes when I was younger! I am reminded of my viewpoint in my younger years as I read a card recently that said, "She packed up her potential and all she had learned, grabbed a cute pair of shoes, and headed out to change a few things." —Leah Stanley

Now I grab the sturdy shoes, but I still head out to change a few things.

Relevancy for the Future

Because of my age, I have sometimes felt like I am in the wrong tour group simply because I am older than those I am with. I feel disconnected or out of sorts and find myself wondering if I am relevant to younger people, if I am even interesting for them to talk to. For the most part, my own ageism gets in the way of believing I have a place. I don't know how it happens, but it does.

As we age there can be a feeling of nearing the end of our road, as if we should be getting ready to be done; when, honestly, that can't be further from the truth. I have not met one person who, as they age, wants to be considered done. In fact, most of those I have met who are fifty-five and older want to continue to feel connected to a larger picture. We want our value to be seen and recognized.

Whether it is technology, trying new careers, new adventures, or even joining tour groups, each will provide a new door to open. Finding what is behind each door is a part of the experience. Sometimes the doors we go through bring us to places of learning, sadness, and gratefulness. Sometimes the doors we go through are not ones we would have selected. They were selected for us. Yet each one holds great value on the other side if we pay attention. We will transition as we open and then close the doors we walk through.

Transitions will likely occur multiple times in a woman's life. If we allow ourselves to see the gift we are afforded by having so many doors to choose from, aging can go from a sign that things are almost over to a sign of things to come! It means we still have the gift of time. Transitions will automatically include changing our beliefs and perspectives around aging.

Neither our age nor our underwear size has anything to do with our ability. It boils down to our beliefs. We have to believe that we have worth, that we have relevance. What we give out is what we will get back. What we have as a perspective about aging is how we will live.

The reality is, we live in a world that values youth more than age and wisdom. As I no longer fit in the youth category, I find I have no bitterness about it, only regret. I regret not engaging more with people older than myself when I was younger. I regret not valuing the experiences my grandparents had and could have given me advice about. I regret not asking earlier in my career for money toward our retirement package!

If I could pass true wisdom along to younger people it would be this: don't be afraid to not know everything. Ask those of us who have been around awhile. Many of us who are older aren't necessarily wiser about everything, but we have had experiences we can all learn from. Seek to understand . . . but first you gotta ask!

A story shared by a woman in one gathering illustrated the value of the perspective we can learn from people who are older. She said, "In my work with the elderly, I developed a friendship with a woman named Lilly Rose. She died two weeks before she turned 108. When she was 105 years old, I decided to interview her. One of the questions I asked her was what was the best day she could remember? Her answer was: the day they brought the outhouse IN the house!"

It's all about perspective.

Something I don't regret as I age is that I am now more able to see the value of people. Not only do I value youth and their vision and ability to get things done, but I also value the wisdom that comes from having experienced a few things along the way. Age allows us to look back and learn from what we accomplished and what we tried to accomplish. If we could balance out the wisdom learned with the risks to be taken, think of all of the wonderful things that could happen! Boy, I wish I could have met myself when I was younger now that I have all this wisdom to pass along!

One of the gifts I give myself is to honor the present and be able to re-imagine myself as I age. Though it can be challenging, we all need to embrace the idea that we are still able to accomplish things like saving for retirement or taking a pottery class. We may view certain ages as markers for what we should have done by now; we lock ourselves into thinking that if we have not accomplished this or that by a certain age, so we should probably say good-bye to wanting it, to ever moving toward it. Well, not anymore! I refuse such thinking. I am still out the door to change a few things!

In gratitude for the many opportunities to (re)learn, (re)discover, (re)imagine, and (re)define, and for being in the wrong tour group. After all, I got this, right?

CHAPTER 7

✳ And in the End . . . ✳

TO "SPARKLE ON" IS a metaphor for how I believe I, and all the women I know and interviewed, are living, no matter our age. It is very clear to me that how fast or how slow we move through this life cannot be measured by movement alone. I met some remarkable women in their eighties who may not be running marathons any time soon, but they are as fast as gazelles when it came to recalling information, brainstorming ideas, and offering wisdom.

To be in the company of so many capable women while writing this book made it even more energizing and exciting for me to get out the important messages about women and aging: Our age means nothing. It is our intentions that hold the meaning and purpose. It is about how we live our life that matters.

My great-grandmother died at age 101. She was a housekeeper well into her nineties. She was one of the most influential women in my life. Her powerful influence had nothing to do with how fast she moved or even her age. It was all about the style and integrity in the way she lived. Every day mattered to her. She was beautiful inside and out until the day she died. She is my greatest example for what aging and women are all about.

As I put together the final manuscript for this book, I became acutely aware from all of the beautiful and wise women I spoke with that aging has both a sense of excitement as well as fear. The excitement comes from a place of freedom. Freedom to do some of those things put off due to raising a family, moving forward in a career, or not having the resources available. Now being older, many women spoke of wanting to travel, take a few classes, try a new career, or simply do a little more nothing for a while.

The sense of fear comes from time and the unknown amount left to us and what could happen within the time left. Women spoke of fearing illness, not having the ability to make as much money, and worries around simply paying for living expenses and healthcare. Yet each who shared a fear also spoke with hope for the future.

As the women shared their stories in every Celebrate Women gathering, I became inspired, hopeful, and excited for what the future still holds for me. I shared tears, laughter, and pure joy as women shared some of their most personal stories.

There is great value in getting together with other women. I felt magic happen each time I attended a Celebrate Women gathering. I was struck over and over with the candidness women offer each other, even when meeting for the first time. Some women brought us into their stories of despair only to lead us to a place of hope and peace. Many shared about still having something to give and were intentional about their giving.

I was reminded of the saying, "A comfort zone is a beautiful place, but nothing ever grows there." —J. Travis.

So true.

I hope this book strongly conveys the message that aging does not mean life is over. The stereotypes of aging need to be challenged and dispelled. In the book *Disrupt Aging*, the CEO of AARP, Jo Ann Jenkins, writes of putting our experiences to work. She asks readers to answer these questions:

What fulfills you?

What are you good at?

What ways of working appeal to you?

What are the opportunities around you?

The premise being that we do not have to be done contributing simply because of our age. That myth is debunked. We hold great relevance as we age.

There will be changes. But those changes do not have to define us. They can challenge us. And based on what I learned from so many women, we can become even stronger. Even wiser. And even happier because of those challenges.

The wisdom I found when speaking with women of a certain age is certainly not tapped into enough. I often wonder what would happen if we allowed women to lead this world.

I believe it would be a much nicer place to live in. Just ask us, and in the meantime, we will sparkle on.

Sparkles of Wisdom

GATHERED FROM WOMEN I INTERVIEWED:

What is something you learned from aging?

- No judging. You never know what someone else has been through to get them to this place.
- Kindness really matters.
- Don't make assumptions about how others feel or why.
- Tolerance is really important.
- Be more compassionate.
- Have patience. You can blow up later if you still want to by then.
- Self-love is most important. If you don't have love for yourself you will look to others to give it to you. It's never all that you want.
- You don't have to be friends with everyone.
- Spend time doing what matters.
- Getting to age along with someone you really enjoy and love is special. Don't take it for granted.

What is something you regret?

- Not getting a formal education. I didn't make it a priority, and I wish I had.
- I didn't travel more.
- I married right out of college. I never knew what it was like to be on my own.
- Following fashion advice from those who I really don't know or care about. I regret not wearing what I wanted to more often.
- I wish I wasn't such a peace-maker. I wore myself out!
- Not knowing how to handle conflict. I still run from it. I don't know why it scares me so.
- I never learned to stand on my own. I wanted to but, getting married so early, I had my husband to rely on and he took care of everything. As a result I always put him first.
- I regret trying to keep the house so clean all the time. I missed out on time with my kids or friends because of cleaning! How stupid was that?
- Worrying too much. I sure wish I knew then what I know now. I would not have worried so much about things I cannot control.
- Not doing more for myself. I love painting, and I never did anything about that when I was younger. You know what? I am going to sign up for a class this week!

What do you find important to celebrate?

- Empty nesting! Love my kids and love it more that they don't live at home anymore!
- Grandchildren. They are the light in my life.
- Loving my grandchildren. When they return that love my heart explodes.
- Each birthday . . . at our age think of the alternative.
- Not having a period anymore.
- Uninterrupted time spent with my husband.
- Trying something new when I feel like it.
- Relationships with older children. I love having a beer with them now!
- Hearing "I love you" at just the right moment.
- Learning how to set up a Facebook page.
- Having my health. I don't hear as well, but the rest of me is doing pretty well.

What is something you do not like about aging?

- Body changes.
- Getting up in front of people, and they rush over to help me.
- Soreness all over and in places I am pretty sure I never moved during the day.

- Joint replacements. I have had two. You would think I would be able to run a marathon by now. I barely walk to the end of the block without needing to take ibuprophen.
- Feeling worn out.
- People ahead of me in age are becoming frail. It's hard to watch.
- Having more losses. Loss of parents, siblings, and other relationships.
- The loss of sex drive and not having a flat stomach.
- Not feeling relevant anymore.
- Being one of the oldest at work. I am not asked for my perspective much anymore.
- My children seem to think I need help more than I do. They feel like the parents and I am the child. Hey, I can still make a great gimlet and win a card game!

What is some sage advice you would like to pass along to younger women?

- Don't clean your house so much.
- Put your phone down. Play with your kids. Pay attention to what is going on around you.
- Have a mentor. Find a woman a step or two ahead of you to ask questions of and seek advice from.
- Communicate with people who are important to you.
- Have courageous conversations if you must. But keep your mouth shut, too.

- Be kinder to yourself.
- Trust your intuition.
- Do not judge others . . . there is ALWAYS a backstory.
- Stop doing things you know do not work.
- Don't be afraid of changes. Some of the best things come from them.
- Try not to be so focused that you end up not contributing.
- There is no age-defying anything. You live a good life, you have a good life.
- Throw away all pantyhose.
- Take chances. It is never too late.
- Don't be afraid to ask for what you want. If you don't get it, go out and find it for yourself.
- Believe there is something greater than yourself.
- Never forget your tweezers, reading glasses, and someone's birthday.
- Leave a little sparkle wherever you go.

These sparkles of wisdom brought to you by women of a certain age. Sparkle on . . .

It is better to look back on life and say,
"I can't believe I did that," than to look back
and say, "I wish I did that."

✳ Acknowledgments ✳

AS A WRITER, I would hope that I could find the words to express my deepest gratitude for all of the people who came in and out of my life while I was writing this book. So many were there helping me, guiding me, or simply just listening. Some people were there for only moments while others were there for my entire writing journey. All had a strong impact on my moving forward. Saying thank you does not seem to encompass the depth of appreciation I feel for everyone who helped to make this book come alive. But that is what I feel—incredibly thankful!

I wish to extend my unconditional gratitude for the women who hosted all of the wonderful "Celebrate Women" gatherings. If not for your willingness to open up your homes, I would have been left with making stuff up. I appreciate that you shared your friends, time, and stories with me. Thank you to all of the women who gathered in a circle over drinks, food, and laughter, wondering what kinds of questions I would ask. Your candid heartfelt answers are what drove my wanting to finish this book. Like you, I wanted all other "women of a certain age" to know they are not alone in the aging process. I hope I captured your sentiment, humor, and perspective as a collective story. We are not alone.

There are a few people I want to specifically thank:

My daughter, Lindsey. Without you, I would have never

been able to complete this book, put together anything involving technology, or finally decide on a book title or cover. I so appreciate that you are just different enough from me that I was able to see things through a slightly different lens when I needed to (not always when I wanted to). Your help, support, and love (and singing) are what, many times, kept me going.

Thank you to my sons, Joe and Ryan. While this is a book about women and aging, something you really do not relate to, your continuous check-ins and "wow moms" meant the world to me. Your selfless excitement for me added to what wonderful young men you are. My cup runneth over with love for you.

To my mom. Your beauty inside and out is something, I noticed, we do not talk about. We should talk about it. While writing this book I had an epiphany that without you, I would not be who I am today. I thank you for all of the times you told me you were proud of me for writing this book. I thank you for being one of my biggest supporters today and for all the todays past and those to come. Thank you.

I have a picture sitting on my shelf that I would look at every time I would write in my office. It is of my sister and me at the zoo goofing around. It is one of my favorite photos. Looking at this photo makes me smile and realize how lucky I am to have a sister who is on my side through thick and thin. You are there for me, no matter if we are referencing life situations or body size. We go way back . . . and I am excited to go way forward with you. *I've got you babe . . .*

Not many of us can say we have a friend since third grade and still really like them . . . but I can. To my bestie, Judith Ann, I cannot possibly write all the thanks I have for you. Suffice it to say there are many stories written in this book that I know you will laugh at, cry from, or get snarky with, all because I have gone through most of them with you! I could not have written a book such as this without your name and our experiences all over it. Honestly, I am at a loss for how to thank you. Just know that this last sentence is written with friendship tears in my eyes and if I were talking with you I could not speak. I think you will know what I mean.

Thank you, Amy Quale, my fabulous publisher extraordinaire. It took going to San Francisco to meet, even though we are both from Minnesota! If ever there was an argument for there are no coincidences . . . this would be one of them. I feel so lucky to have met you and then be able to work with you. Thank you for your kind style of helping me put together the very best writing I could muster up. You are very good at what you do. This is a placeholder to write those powerful words I can't seem to find to express my gratitude . . . until then, thank you.

Without getting too schmaltzy, there are so many others to whom I would like to express my gratitude. Without even one of you, this project would never have been completed. Thank you to those who read my book in its various stages, with the typos, weird grammar, and sentences that did not flow. I appreciated your suggestions; I was sometimes embarrassed, but I always appreciated your help (except that one time and you know who you are).

An especially big and heartfelt thank you to Stephanie. Even now, I think of you as the coauthor. Remember meeting at the coffee shop and starting the conversation about this book? Well . . . we did it! Let's go back to the coffee shop and have a toast . . . and talk about the next book!

It appears I could probably write a book about just thanking people. I really do feel indebted to so many people's support, gifts of time, feedback, encouragement, prayers, and "pick-ups" when I was down and thought this was a stupid idea to write a book. To all of those whose names would fill a book, I can only hope that if you need anything from me, you will ask. I am feeling verklempt at the moment, so this would be a good time to ask.

"You don't have to see where you're going, you don't have to see your destination or everything you will pass along the way. You just have to see two or three feet ahead of you."
—Anne Lamott

Thanks to all who kept pushing me two or three feet at a time to complete this book.

Sparkle on . . .

✶ About the Author ✶

KIM KANE is a speaker, blogger, writer, and a woman of a certain age. She has lived more than she will . . . and while she isn't thrilled about this, she does intend to look at life as still filled with opportunities to take advantage of.

Kim has worked with youth and families experiencing difficulties for the past thirty years. She describes the work as exhausting, exhilarating, and humbling all at the same time. Working with youth has helped keep her perspective young. However, she is reminded she is aging when trying to find underwear that fits *and* feels comfortable.

In her fantasy life, Kim and her husband are living on a lake with a couple of dogs. Her house is in the north woods where it seems like fall every day and she drinks her coffee on her deck every morning to the lullaby of the loons singing. And she writes.

In her real life, Kim continues to work with youth and families, lives with her husband in a suburb of Minneapolis, and has one dog. Currently, her kitchen is gutted for a remodel and she cannot find her favorite spatula or the salt. And she writes. *Sparkle On* is her first book.

To connect with Kim, visit:
Blog: KimKaneandGratitude.com
Facebook: @LivingLifeinTandem
Twitter: @Aging_Gratitude